Sales Craft

Proven Tips, Tactics and Ideas
to Elevate Your Sales Success

Sales
Craft

Sales Craft

Proven Tips, Tactics and Ideas
to Elevate Your Sales Success

Brendan McAdams

Kiinetics Press

ISBN: 9781686998898

Produced by Kiinetics Press
www.brendanmcadams.com
Cover design by author and Mark Loraditch
Icons used on the cover and internal pages provided by Freepik from flaticon.com

You're an experienced sales professional on the lookout for new skills or a fresh perspective. Or perhaps you're just getting started in sales and looking to get up to speed as quickly as possible.

In either case, this book was written for you. It's a collection of observations, practices and techniques that have proven invaluable to my sales success.

You may not agree with all of them, and you may find some of them obvious or intuitive. But if you're like me, you're always looking for one more good idea and one more chance to get better. Some practical, incremental ways to raise your game and hone your craft. I'm confident you'll find a few in the pages that follow.

TABLE OF CONTENTS

Introduction

Let me start by explaining what this book isn't. It isn't a richly detailed, step-by-step sales scheme for transforming you into the next sales superstar. And you won't find a systematic, five phase sales methodology here either. There are plenty of those sorts of resources out there. And chances are you've already got a sales process.

Instead, this book is a compilation of the various sales techniques and observations that I've collected, tested, evaluated and ultimately adopted over the course of my sales career. Some are simple and perhaps even pedantic, and others may come off as philosophical ramblings, but all of them have served me well over the years. My hope is that you'll experiment with them and find them worth adding to your own sales repertoire.

Sales Craft is about fundamentals and habits. Like having the footwork required to be a good boxer or the knife skills that make a good chef, it's knowing the basics and then executing them. Consistently and deftly.

Becoming good at anything requires practice, attention to detail, constant refinement and continuous learning. And being good at sales is no different. Expertise comes slowly, over time and often in frustratingly small increments. At least that has been my experience. Much of what I write about focuses on those little increments, partly because they add up and partly because they don't get the attention and use that they warrant. My hope is that you find *Sales Craft* to be both approachable and thought-provoking.

You'll notice that it's organized into three major sections: *Essentials*, *Extras*, and *The Mental Game*. *Essentials* covers some basic sales practices that should be part of every regimen, while *Extras* focuses on next-level sales techniques worth considering. Finally, *The Mental Game* is a big picture examination of the sales profession and how to think about one's place in it. From my perspective, being a professional salesperson is one of the truly ideal career choices and so deserves rigorous thought, contemplation and an adherence to one's convictions.

That said, feel free to jump to any page or section. It's intended as a reference, and maybe as a reminder to regularly add to or reinforce good sales habits.

The pages ahead are an admittedly incomplete list of basic tips, practices and ideas that have worked for me. And I expect to add to this list at www.brendanmcadams.com, and invite you to pass along suggestions as well.

Lastly, this book is meant as a small repayment to the profession that has been so good to me over the years. In no other job could I have experienced so much, met so many good people or been allowed the sort of creative outlet that selling has given me. As a good friend and an expert salesperson once summarized so effectively about his career choice, "It's a good thing the world needs guys like me, because I'm not qualified to do anything else."

I genuinely hope that you find the observations and suggestions here to be valuable and motivational as you continue to develop your craft.

Happy selling!

Brendan McAdams
September 2019

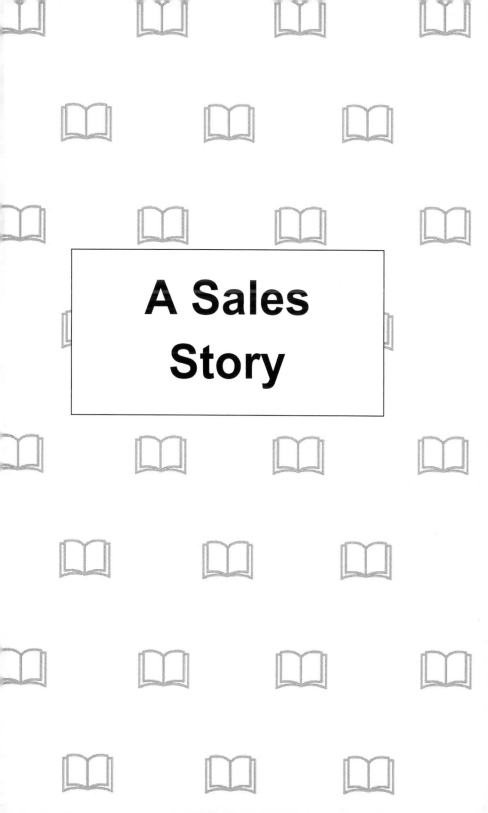

A Sales Story

6

A Sales Story

Let's start with some background.

We're Not in Hollywood

If you stick with selling long enough, you'll eventually get a chance to pitch your first really big deal. Perhaps it promises huge revenue, or has strategic importance for the company, or it involves an important presentation to a room of senior executives, or just has the potential to really blow out the comp plan. Whatever the circumstances, it's a simultaneously thrilling and humbling experience, and when you're in the midst of such a deal it can feel truly overwhelming. But it can also offer a moment of clarity, because you come face-to-face with the realization that being a professional salesperson is either just a job or, hopefully, something much bigger.

My first significant sales opportunity had all of the above ingredients. It was big (relatively speaking), amounting to about thirty percent of my quota. It was lucrative, in that it would put me over quota and into some attractive accelerators. It was strategic to the company as it would set us up as the standard database software and programming tools for the client organization, which meant a big dog-and-pony presentation before any purchase decision could occur. Plus, it all had to get done by midnight on December 31st. (One of the odd realities of working for a public company is the arbitrary deadline of the fiscal year end.)

To get this deal closed, we needed to set up a detailed technical presentation and proposal discussion with a key executive director of this Fortune Ten company. This particular executive had signing authority for millions of dollars, had a global organization with over 10,000 people reporting up through him, and had a well-deserved reputation for being impatient, demanding, and painfully blunt. We needed a commitment by the middle of December if we were going to get all the paperwork done and the deal closed and booked.

It wasn't easy. After what seemed like a never-ending coordination campaign, juggling calendars to make sure all the right people were available, we had a date set: 5:00pm on a Thursday one week before Christmas. I spent weeks leading up to this big event editing and updating slide decks and proposals, both internally and with my day-to-day contact. I also spent hours fine-tuning the value proposition, addressing the potential obstacles and outlining the technical support structure.

Every day seemed to uncover some new problem or concern. An inexplicable bug turned up in the software that caused their system to hang. One of the client's engineers had an intense encounter with our tech support team. Their team of attorneys raised possible deal-killing licensing issues. AS these piled up, the likelihood of the big pitch meeting was looking less encouraging with each passing day.

Truthfully, I'd started to hope the big day would never arrive. My boss was one of those 'hands-off, throw you into the deep end, what doesn't kill you makes you stronger' kind of sales managers. Which meant I owned everything start to finish. Every detail leading up to the presentation, the presentation materials, all the prep coordination, all the proposal details, and even making the presentation itself were all in the hands of someone totally out of his depth. Me.

Every aspect of this effort was new territory. I'd never structured a multi-year, global, value-added reseller proposal before. I hadn't dealt with our headquarters on any non-standard performance thresholds. I had no prior experience working with our product management and engineering teams to influence the prioritization of specific features. Most terrifying of all, this would be my first time making a complex and financially-significant proposal presentation to a conference room filled with senior executives.

Finally, that fateful Thursday in December arrived. My boss and I were at the client's headquarters well before 5 pm to wait, first in the main lobby before being greeted and ushered up so we could then wait in the boardroom. The room itself seemed to intensify the already crippling dread that had been building in me over the last several days. It was a huge and imposing space, with impressive paneling, automatic shades to close off the view, projection screens that would lower from the ceiling with the touch of a button, and dozens of expensive chairs surrounding a table the size of a respectable boat.

My nervous pacing, paper shuffling and various other tics must have been noticeable to my otherwise detached boss, causing him to smile and let out a small chuckle. "You know," he said with some mild amusement, "there will be a day when you look back on this as just the first of many multi-million-dollar deals in your career." I don't remember how I responded, if at all, because it was then that my client and several members of his team poured into the boardroom, greeted us quickly and then explained that the executive director was running late and that we should get started.

After quick pleasantries and determining the appropriate seating arrangement in such an oversized room, I launched into the presentation in a rushed but semi-competent manner.

About ten minutes into my presentation, the executive director swept into the room with a serious flourish, grabbed one of the many extra handouts set out ahead of time, and headed for what must have been his usual seat near the far end of the table. I stopped. The room became heavy and still, which prompted him to raise his hand in a rolling gesture and say "Keep going." This was a practice he was evidently accustomed to. He then turned his attention back to the handout and proceeded to page his way through.

I did as I was instructed, my presentation now lurching along even more nervously than before, but only until it was interrupted a few short minutes later. The executive director unceremoniously collected his handout, got up from his seat, glanced quickly at my main contact with a look that I couldn't interpret and swept out as briskly as he had arrived.

I completed the remaining slides with a feeling not unlike being down twenty points in the big game with three minutes left, the win impossibly out of reach but the clock still needing to be played out. When we finally wrapped up the meeting, it was with the standard platitudes and perfunctory post-game conversation, except that I had no idea if we'd won or lost. But from where I was standing, it definitely felt like defeat.

Because it was now Thursday evening and my client wouldn't speak with the executive director until the following week, the impending doom would cloud the weekend. We could do nothing but wait for the inevitable bad news. So we waited. Until December 30th, when the office fax machine buzzed to life with a purchase order that reflected exactly the proposal terms we'd made in the presentation.

It was several weeks later, after the holidays passed and we were well into the new project, when my client explained what happened. The meeting was a formality, a required milestone after all the real work had been done. He explained casually that the decision was essentially made days prior, the team and senior management having been made comfortable with the deal and confident in their vendor selection as a result of the run-up to the meeting. It turned out the executive director had already seen the presentation, perhaps even a better delivered version, so why sit through it again? We'd already won. We just didn't know it. (Or at least I didn't.) No fanfare or big reveal. Anti-climactic.

My reaction was mostly surprise, tinged with a mild sense of anger that I'd gone through weeks of preparation, angst and self-doubt for nothing. Just think of the time and effort saved if they'd been transparent about the process. Maybe I expected that the meeting would wrap up with a dramatic close, after which the executive director would clear his throat and say, "Excellent! Let's get going with this right away," followed by handshakes and vigorous back-slapping and congratulations.

Of course, that would have been the wrong lesson to take away. Yes, any good story benefits from a big finish, something with lots of noise and excitement and revelation. But that's Hollywood. If this experience taught me anything, it's that real life and real sales situations generally don't work like that.

Rather, it's keeping up the grind. Executing on the fundamentals. Continuing to show up. Adding to your set of skills. Giving serious thought to what you do and how you do it. Day after day refining your craft.

Which isn't a bad thing. It just means that all the worry and fear is wasted energy, and the mundane day-in, day-out stuff may not feel like you're living inside a major motion picture. But that doesn't mean it won't have its dramatic moments.

You just want to be ready when they happen.

Essentials

Essentials

Fundamentals. Basic blocking and tackling.
Practical habits that work.

Starting Out

Early in any career, there is a lack experience, wisdom and industry knowledge. That's to be expected. But in its place there should be plenty of something else: energy, work ethic, curiosity and character. The best advice I can share is to use those qualities to their fullest early and often.

Don't overthink things, and don't prepare excessively. Instead, dive in. Make calls, make appointments, make presentations and make mistakes. If you make lots of the first three, you'll make plenty of the last. Which is inevitable. Learning and experience typically accumulate through failure and error; real accomplishments seldom occur without them. Own up to them, learn from them and then move forward.

To their credit, most people are surprisingly quick to forgive mistakes, even sizable ones, if made with good intentions and ethics. Just apologize to the victims with genuine, sincere conviction and keep going. It's actually reassuring to witness how tolerant and even encouraging people tend to be to those who make big, bold, creative errors.

Ideally, you're in a job with a company and a boss that understand the value inherent in trying. If you're not, maybe it's time to move on. Because the way to accumulate that experience, wisdom and industry knowledge is to pour yourself into the job, learn as much as you can as quickly as you can, and make a bunch of mistakes along the way.

So, dive in.

After the Interview

So you've aced the interview and all that comes after it. Now they are preparing to offer you the job. Let's take a minute to cover a couple 'surprises' that never seem to get any attention but that are as reliable as the next sunrise.

The first of these is the elapsed time between "We like you and we're going to offer you the job" and actually getting the offer letter itself.

It will seem ridiculously long for someone eager for confirmation and looking to dive in. It could easily be a week and just as likely two or three. Or longer.

And the waiting will be miserable. You're in limbo. You've decided, at least in your head, but it's not really mutual yet. It's

21

like that awkward gap after you've finally summoned up the courage to say that first, hopeful 'I love you' but the only thing that follows is a long, excruciating silence.

Hey, there's no point in worrying. Most companies (and people) just slow down after they've made a big decision. Maybe it's tiring, or they feel like they've enough work for that week. Nobody really knows why. Just relax. You'll get the offer. Go celebrate.

Which bring us to something you probably *should* worry about. What happens once you start.

There's an excellent chance that the job you interview for won't be the job you end up doing. It won't be the territory you were promised, or with the job title, or the compensation plan. You may not even end up working for the manager you interviewed with and thought you'd be reporting to.

I can't explain why this happens nor can I offer a good solution when it happens, but the chances of it happening to you at some point in your career (and more than once) are really good. Easily better than 50:50. I know because they've all happened to me, and I consider myself pretty lucky.

All I can suggest is this: Be prepared. Try to uncover as many of the potential pitfalls during the interview process. Walk through a few 'theoretical' scenarios, explain past job surprises that you'd rather not relive, get as much of the job description in writing as possible.

It won't completely eliminate the possibility of a significant career surprise. But should improve your odds.

Five Things to Anticipate in a Sales Presentation

1. It will take longer than you thought to sign in at security, and the client's office will be at the far end of the building.

2. The audio/video process requires them to call in someone 'from IT.'

3. Because something has 'come up,' there's a hard stop 30 minutes earlier than scheduled.

4. There's some mystery person in attendance.

5. The client now wants to 'start things off with a few slides' (that you haven't seen.)

Being on Time

Be on time.

Show up on time. Arrive promptly for all meetings, events, conference calls, webinars, every customer interaction. Even better, arrive a few minutes early. Make it a habit. Few efforts telegraph respect and professionalism more quietly and effectively than being on time.

Obvious stuff, but it happens less often than you'd think.

This is basic, stick-to-the-knitting sort of advice. (Skip ahead if you're already on top of this.) Yet it's one of the many little efforts that create the impression from which customers operate and form their opinions. We may think that purchase decisions are made solely on important product features and functions, but that supposes that human beings are consistently rational and logical.

They aren't. At least not consistently. Emotional factors play a huge role. And simple, seemingly trivial details can have outsized importance. Things like "She returns calls right away," "He shows up on time," or "She helps me look like I know what I'm doing."

Being on time becomes an even bigger challenge when you're herding a crowd, but that only makes it that much more important. The big meeting simply demands more planning: for the time-suck of calling and getting a hold of your sponsor, for signing in, for security inspections, for the mile-long walk from lobby to conference room, for setting up A/V equipment and the inevitable troubleshooting that follows, etc. But make it organized and productive and you're on your way to establishing real credibility and an even better impression.

If you really want the deal, and the deal that comes after that one, you'll make the effort. Set an alarm, include a cushion for delays and unforeseen circumstances, or take a course in time management. Do whatever it takes.

Just be there.

Being Late

You will be late. It may even be unavoidable. The birth of a child, a death in the family, a flat tire. These things happen. Life has a way of making things complicated.

As soon as you know and it is practical to do so, let your client know. This is the real reason cell phones and text messaging were invented. An email or phone call twenty minutes before your scheduled time saying you're running ten minutes late is far better than just showing up late. For both you *and* your client.

At a minimum, your customer won't be hanging around wondering where the heck you are. They might even consider this free time as a gift and a chance to catch up on something.

Yes, this change in circumstances presents the opportunity for your customer to reschedule, or even cancel. It's possible. But if a particular incident causes them to blow you off, perhaps they weren't qualified in the first place. (Or maybe they're just tired of your consistently inconsiderate inability to show up on time?)

Whatever the case, make the call as soon as you can. If you're calling the administrative assistant, you might get some help juggling things around, but make the call regardless. Apologize. Offer to reschedule. Have alternative dates and times in mind. Be apologetic for the inconvenience, but you don't need to grovel.

But you better show up next time.

Time is Money

Time has value. We spend time. Of course, we want to be efficient with our own time. Just as important, it makes good sense to be similarly conscientious with our prospect's time. And that respect for a customer's time can take shape in any number of ways.

Because email has become so central with our sales efforts, it deserves particular attention. Emails should be brief and limited to just the necessary number of sentences to get the point across without extraneous rambling. Use the Albert Einstein rule when it comes to email – "Everything should be made as simple as possible, but not simpler."

Format your messages for easy reading -- and if there's a response needed, the need is clearly explained and the required response apparent. Use a bulleted list to make a necessarily longer message more digestible and easier for the reader to process.

If you're just sharing something simple, fit it in the subject line with a trailing (EOM), as in End of Message. If you've got a lot to cover across multiple topics, it probably makes sense to break it up into multiple messages with a quick explanation that you will cover these details in another email. This approach allows the client to digest and respond in chunks at their convenience and on their schedule.

Phone calls deserve similar attention. If they're unscheduled (interruptions), make it clear that you'll be brief and just want to cover A and B. Of course, this obligates you to be brief, so plan accordingly. The definition of 'brief' varies by customer, with thirty seconds of pleasantries a lifetime for some clients and five minutes of "How're the kids?" a completely reasonable time span for others. Yes, you can yak away about last night's Yankees-Giants game for as long as the client is enthusiastically engaged. But be highly attuned to the subtle signals that it's time to move on to the real business of the call.

Overall, a brisk and concise treatment of the call's objective is a good strategy. It conveys seriousness and that you're busy, too. You can always follow up with an equally concise email summary, if appropriate.

Economy of time is especially important with scheduled calls and meetings. Don't ask for an hour unless you really need it. You'd be surprised what can be discussed and resolved in thirty minutes, or even less. Plus, you'll get a lot more access to prospective customers if your request is, "Can we get ten minutes to talk about X?" Who has sixty minutes to burn anymore, especially anyone responsible for significant purchasing decisions? Hour-long meetings and phone calls should be reserved for product demonstrations and events that generate lots of questions.

If you have to ask for an hour, make the request with "and we should be able to get it wrapped up quicker." And then wrap it up quickly. For busy executives, there are few surprises that are more pleasantly received than getting back twenty minutes of their day.

Customers will quickly recognize you as someone who doesn't waste time, either theirs or your own. You're seen as a professional focused on being efficient and considerate. Most customers can free up ten or twenty minutes to discuss something important. As long as it's important, and as long as it's less than ten or twenty minutes.

Five Travel Tips for the Stressed Sales Pro

1. Headphones and ear plugs

2. Keep a file of reading materials (e.g. articles, blog posts) to read on the plane.

3. On long flights, sitting at the back puts you closer to the bathroom. On short flights, sitting towards the front gets you off the plane faster.

4. When checking into a hotel, ask for something (e.g. a good view, extra room, a quiet section, something nice.) It almost always pays off.

5. Carry an auxiliary battery. (Ideally, it can recharge a laptop as well as your phone.)

Be Reliable

One of the most basic rules for a successful sales career is to do what you say you're going to do. You could also argue it's the most obvious. (It's also a rule that translates equally well to most other areas of life.) In two words, be reliable.

Deliver on your commitments. Be on time. Make sure your customer gets the document or other obligation you promised when (or before) you promised it. Failing to deliver on time causes a cascade of potential responses, from irritation to frustration to resignation to disqualification. None of them are good and all of them avoidable. When unplanned delays occur that jeopardize the delivery, advanced warning helps. It's rare that you don't know well beforehand that something is not on schedule, so there's seldom a reason not to give your client the heads-up.

Own your mistakes. Be quick to admit an error. A mistake early in the sales cycle is a harder spot to dig out from than one late in the process when you'd had the chance to establish a reputation for professional follow-thorough. This might cause some hesitation, thinking you can let it slide. It's better to own it. The customer may be disappointed, and even angry, but is ultimately likely to appreciate the update. More importantly, it's psychically liberating for you almost from the moment you deliver the news. Try it and you'll see.

The key ingredient necessary to make this rule easier to follow is to be mindful, even cautious, about what you promise and when you promise it. For example, don't offer to send them a proposal tomorrow if it means writing it up from scratch, requires complex configuration help from others, and/or depends on management approval before you can share it. (Of course, this is where your Sales Toolkit can help. See page 49.) Similarly, don't tell them you'll be there in thirty minutes when it's a twenty-minute drive and you're standing in your bedroom, taking the call in your underwear.

Most of the time, your client's expectations are less demanding than your own, affording you room to maneuver. Give yourself some cushion. It's infinitely easier to be reliable, punctual and responsive when you've got time to work with. But once you've committed, do what you can to stick to your promises.

Over time, this sort of follow-through becomes habit-forming. And as one of the most basic habits you need to be successful in sales, it makes everything else that much easier.

Don't Be Too Reliable

Of course you should follow up, be professional, and have clients feel comfortable that you can be counted on. But that doesn't mean you can't occasionally find ways to amuse or (pleasantly) surprise your customers.

Maybe that means sending over pizza or handing out gifts to the crew. I have hot sauce with 'Pour on the Heat' and my logo emblazoned on the bottle as atypical swag. When I was selling to AT&T, I would hand out hundreds of pocket protectors made for the engineers at Bell Labs.

Doing the unexpected has a unique and outsized power that is both disarming and fun to be a part of. Make a point of doing the risky, unexpected, crazy thing on occasion. Comfort and predictability are overrated.

It's great to be reliable. Just find ways to do it without being dull. Look for little ways to set yourself apart. A little unpredictability properly applied is a reliable way to separate yourself from the crowd.

The Other Elevator Pitch

I happened to share an elevator with two sales guys leaving a sales call. (I think they sold disaster recovery software.) On the long descent, these two proceeded to discuss their disappointing sales presentation, going so far as to badmouth a particular engineering manager at that company. With that manager's associate, from the same department, in the elevator. It's not hard to imagine that getting back to the wrong person.

Similarly, it's common to overhear salespeople talking about a deal or a client or some organizational change in the cafeteria, hallway or lobby. It never fails to amaze me what you might inadvertently learn in public settings.

Obviously, be selective about what you say when you're on

customer premises. Elevators and bathrooms seem to invite confidential disclosures that are better kept to yourself until you're out of the building.

There's a tremendous urge to do a detailed post-mortem with your peers the very minute you leave the conference room or get wrapped up in a congratulatory celebration complete with high fives and fist bumps as you make your way to the elevator. Hold off.

Complaining, call summaries, impolitic observations, off-color jokes and strategy discussion should wait until you are in the parking lot. Or your car. Or your office.

Definitely not in their elevator.

Find Your Authenticity

It's time we got a little touchy-feely.

People want to buy from people they like, trust and can identify with. And those same people can pretty much figure out if they like, trust and can identify with you. In a few minutes. And if that's true, how can one possibly prepare themselves for that immediate assessment?

Be authentic.

Good salespeople figure out who they are, what makes them tick, how they think and work and act. They then use that fully informed sense of self as the basis for who they are as a salesperson (and as a person.) They're authentic. And that authenticity is unique and immediately identifiable.

Customers want a genuine experience, and are justifiably repelled from experiences that feel fake or contrived. When people look to make big decisions in either their professional or personal life, the overwhelming and totally natural tendency is to deal with people they view as trustworthy, genuine and real. (It's actually hardwired into our DNA.) Certainly, there are situations where people decide against their gut or their self-interest, but those are the very same decisions that most readily get unwound or contested later.

The fake, slimy salesperson is so common that it's its own cliché. Perhaps the penultimate example is Alec Baldwin's 'Coffee is for Closers' soliloquy (or tirade) in *Glengarry Glen Ross*, which has a disheartening 3.5 million YouTube views. One can only hope those views are to remind us sales professionals what *not* to do.

The world is rife with those who sacrifice their identity, succumb to peer pressure against their better judgment, or otherwise can't muster the effort to be who they want to be. There's even a decent chance that your customer is struggling with his or her own authenticity issues, so maybe yours will inspire them.

In my own case, I figured out years ago that I can't be serious 100% of the time. Or 80%. (Truthfully, 50% is a struggle.) Now I just embrace that and take my licks when I run up against a customer who is serious 24x7. They either warm up (or frown and bear it), or they go a different route. Because the minute I can't yuck it up or laugh off some idiosyncratic aspect of my sales style is the exact minute it becomes drudgery. And who wants that?

Customers don't. At least not in my experience. They may act like they want someone who's all business and serious as a grand jury investigation, but don't bet on it. I've sold to customers as serious as CMS (the Medicare/Medicaid folks in the US government) and engineers designing anti-submarine warfare systems, and they like a good laugh and a relaxed, collegial environment as much as the next customer.

Of course, if you're one of those people that is genuinely all business, always have all your ducks in a row, and aren't wired to appreciate the absurdity of the human condition, you need to embrace that 100%. Because that's you. It's what you've been dealt. And until it's not, it's the best hand you've got. (This is a great time to suggest the cinematic classic *Harold and Maude* as the antidote to *Glengarry Glen Ross*, BTW.)

Ultimately, customers find it liberating to deal with someone who is who they say they are. The contracting is easier and more accommodating, the due diligence is inevitably less rigorous, the paperwork and the process more flexible. An unspoken understanding occurs when the client has the opportunity to work with an authentic salesperson. You stand a greater chance of winning simply because you represent yourself accurately. And it sets you apart because it's so hard for so many of our sales brethren to pull off.

Except it's not that hard. You just have to be you.

Five Familiar
Conference Call Comments

1.　"I didn't get the invite. Can you send it again?"

2.　"I'm sorry but it's not on my calendar."

3.　"I dialed in but nobody else was on."

4.　"A demo? But I'm driving. I just thought it was a phone call."

5.　"We can't get this to work. Let's reschedule?"

Can We Be Honest?

Be blunt, be direct and be honest. Even brutally honest. But don't feel compelled to act this way because it's the right thing to do. Do it because it's effective and expedient. Do it because it's easier to remember. Do it because it saves time. Do it because it's disarming and unexpected.

Honesty is a corollary of authenticity. But honesty should be easier to pull off. We're wired to be honest and have some inherent sensor that tell us when someone is being untruthful. (Authenticity is tougher to pull off because the social pressures to conform are more insidious.)

As salespeople, we're constantly faced with situations where it would seem that the easy, expedient and lucrative option is to bend (or completely break) the truth. After all, it makes the product sound better, it makes you look better and more accommodating, and because it's often what (you think) the customer wants to hear.

Except none of that is true. Let's assume that your career, reputation and legacy are being measured over a span of years rather than that of one deal. In that case, being honest with customers is a better, more lucrative strategy. Customers remember. Word gets around. Plus, you and your fellow employees won't be burdened with trying to support any unattainable claims or promises.

Most importantly, it's tough to be genuinely good at something if not staying within the rules. People prefer a fair, well-played contest. And we feel somehow swindled when one player or team gains an unfair advantage by circumventing the rules. Resorting to falsehoods and misrepresentations means you're no longer selling. Instead, you're just cheating.

Ultimately, excellence in any endeavor is its own reward. Yes, excellent salespeople arguably sell bigger and better deals. Those successes generally lead to more money, which can be excellent, too. But I'm here to suggest that, as trite and predictable as it may sound, the real reward is in the execution.

You can't cheat your way to excellence.

Tech Support

I hate waiting. Standing in line for anything is torture. As is being kept on hold. I can do it, and I consider myself relatively patient. (Others may not agree.) But when it comes to computer work, waiting is misery. And money.

If you're a typical salesperson, you spend a lot of time in front of a computer screen. (Too much, probably.) If you're anything like me, it's mostly internet browsing, email, staring at a CRM, crafting PowerPoint presentations, or working on the occasional spreadsheet. Whatever you're doing, my guess is that you'd probably prefer to get it over with as quickly as possible.

Give some serious thought to the machine you're using.

Chances are that you deserve something better. Honestly, I'm a recent convert to this perspective and the epiphany was long overdue.

I recently made a significant upgrade. I'm not exaggerating when I say it has changed my life.

Here's the pitch: Invest in a good computer. The difference between a decent laptop and a really good one may only be a few hundred dollars, but the dividend that additional investment pays out can be enormous.

This is especially true if a big chunk of that investment is in computer memory (Random Access Memory, or RAM). Today's internet browsers all now have a standard tab feature. I customarily have a couple different browsers open with fifteen (or more) tabs open in each. (Who uses bookmarks anymore?)

The problem is that all these tabs eat up huge chunks of your machine's memory and, and the overall performance suffers as a result. Which means you're waiting for pages to load, refresh and even transition among tabs. Having a lot of RAM helps reduce the waiting.

The same is true with large spreadsheets, or video editing, or ponderously fat PowerPoint presentations. They, too, can eat up your machine's limited memory. A faster processor, solid state hard drive and a dedicated graphics card also help. (More on that in a moment.)

The math is simple. Add up the time you spend waiting for your computer to boot up, load pages, complete complex Excel macros, etc. in a given week and then multiply it by how much your time is worth. (BTW, do you know how much your time is worth? That's a topic for a future blog post.)

Just having the awareness that your machine has you idling is half the exercise. I guarantee you that the cost should have you heading off to Best Buy or scouring the web faster than you can say Kingston PC3-10600R Registered ECC Server RAM.

But before you set off on a shopping spree, let me make a more radical suggestion. Rather than try to upgrade your laptop's resources or buy a new one, consider assigning it to 'travel-only' status and buy yourself a used desktop machine.

Of course, this makes less sense if you're constantly on the road. But if you work primarily from home or a remote office and spend most of your time at the same place, buying a well-configured but lightly used machine can change your life.

I know what you're thinking. "Who buys a ten-year-old computer?" This guy does.

Let me geek out on you for just a moment. It is brain-dead simple to find a machine that has a processor way more powerful and with way more memory than any laptop you can expect to buy, and with a dedicated graphics card and gobs more storage. For less than $400. Yes, the machine will be five to ten years old, but these are workstations and servers that were built for incredibly complex work like CAD/CAM and video editing, and probably cost several thousand dollars new.

The machine I bought for $370, including shipping, has 32GB of RAM, a 2GB graphics card and two hard drives. That same machine originally cost over $8,800 when it was churning through elaborate 3-D rendering or complex statistical models. It can certainly handle my 32-slide presentation and a few dozen browser tabs.

With a home workstation setup, you can then easily configure an existing laptop for travel. Just mirror to a shared Dropbox, Google Drive, or whatever your cloud storage preference may be. Then duplicate any critical apps you might need, and you're off to the races. Plus, you now have a backup machine should you find yourself in the midst of any sort of computer disaster

Take it from someone with direct experience, from one impatient salesperson to another. Make the upgrade and you'll never go back.

Your Sales Toolkit

Because a salesperson's income is directly linked to their sales performance, being more productive pays real dividends. An increase in preparedness and productivity typically translates into an increase in sales success, which should then result in greater earnings. (Or it should.) A ten percent increase in your productivity should result in a ten percent increase in your income, right?

In order to see that kind of consistent return, it helps to have certain processes and practices in place. And one of the most fundamental is creating, managing and updating a sales toolkit.

So, what exactly is a sales toolkit?

Sales Craft

Basically, your sales toolkit is whatever you customarily need to address any significant aspect of the sales process. You will want this core set of sales resources immediately available at the various stages of the sales cycle. In a real sense, your sales ability is evident by what's in your sales toolkit and how well you implement each of these tools. Having the right tools at the ready and using them effectively is critically important to your success.

Your toolkit is the collection of resources required throughout the sales process, from initial engagement through the post-contract phase. This list includes, but is not limited to:

SALES TOOLKIT*

- Marketing Materials: sales collateral, press releases, case studies, references, event schedules
- Sales Documents: discovery documents, call planning sheets, NDA, draft proposals, boilerplate contracts, technical specs
- Implementation Materials: requirements documents, draft Statements of Work, project plans, timelines
- Communications: thank you letters/emails, follow up emails, meeting agendas
- Presentations: branded PowerPoint deck, standard slides on your company, testimonials
- Giveaways: promotional materials like t-shirts, thank you gifts
- Anything else that you routinely need in your sales process

These are the resources that should be immediately accessible and ready to edit and share, either when the client wants them or when it best complements your selling situation.

Consider this. You're no different than the doctor performing an important surgical procedure. The physician's toolkit naturally includes an extensive set of scalpels, rakes, sponges, sutures and an array of even more specialized and esoteric tools laid out and available in anticipation of any possible medical situation. In the same way, you should have your set of prepared resources ready and up-to-date for the inevitable moment when they will be called into duty. (Hey, if you're not able to respond properly when you need to, your deal could *die…*)

Ask yourself these questions:

- What sales materials do I need at each point along the sales process?
- What communications do I use?
- What templates can I use to communicate quickly with prospects and clients?
- What presentations do I use over and over?

Start by first identifying your key resources. Examine your sales process to determine what tools you have and what you may be lacking. Gather the good stuff, create draft versions of the documents you regularly need but don't have, and then move everything else off to the side where it won't be a distraction or get in the way.

Once you've got your set of tools created and collected, it is time to figure out a usable, reliable organizational structure that works for your sales style.

Do you make everything templates and stored documents inside your CRM (customer relationship management software)? This has the advantage of reliability and a record of what has been sent to whom. Or do you create a logical set of folders in Dropbox or Google Drive? This has the advantage of being accessible, sendable, even editable from your cell phone. Or are you truly old-school, and paper-based? There's something to be said for having physical copies of things in an age of electronic clutter that slips off the screen and thus out of the client's attention.

Whatever works for you and whatever your system happens to be, it pays to review it from time to time. During this review, you should add new documents and templates and cull outdated or less effective material to prevent them being a distraction or sent inadvertently.

Remember that the primary objective in developing and maintaining your toolkit is 1) to make you more responsive to your clients, and 2) to make you more efficient. Whenever you can deliver more quickly on your commitments and create a sense of responsiveness and reliability over the course of the sales cycle, you're enhancing both your competitive advantage and your productivity. Ultimately, your goal is to compress time and advance the sales cycle (and your position in it) by having the right tools at hand when you need them.

* Visit brendanmcadams.com to download toolkit samples and templates.

10,000 Hours

Malcolm Gladwell's book, *Outliers*, has one especially famous and often repeated idea. It's where he illustrates the point that anyone who is any good at anything commits a lot of time to that thing. Basically, Gladwell reports that it takes about 10,000 hours to excel at something. Yes, 10,000 hours. As in about five years of a 40-hour-a-week job.

Now apply this idea to your profession. The goal is to work really hard to hit that 10,000 hour mark as soon as possible. Make calls, read books, study the industry, develop contacts. Each of these efforts, including any mistakes made along the way, add up. Before you know it, you will have eclipsed the 10,000-hour threshold.

In that process, something obvious occurs. Things get a little easier. Presentations flow more smoothly. Fewer questions surprise you, and your responses are more polished and effective. Ultimately, deals become more predictable and more manageable.

Ultimately, the real idea behind dedicating 10,000 hours is a focus on continuous incremental improvement. Any 1% improvement is negligible in and of itself. But pile a bunch of 1% improvements one on top of another, day-in and day-out, and the result is staggering. (James Clear's book, *Atomic Habits*, does an excellent job examining this concept.) By taking a 10,000 hour perspective, those daily investments have a chance to compound into an irreplaceable body of expertise and experience.

That's the real takeaway here. Work on the next hour and the 10,000 hours will manage itself. Nuance, finesse, technique, gut feel, and competence are the byproduct of effort invested. One hour at a time. Amassing 10,000 hours isn't a bad way to think about that investment.

A better one may be to focus on the hour you find yourself in.

Call to Confirm

A small but important detail, and a (simple) habit worth adopting, is to confirm your appointments the day prior. The message can be as simple as a one-line email mentioning that you're looking forward to the conversation, or you can shoot over a revised copy of the agenda or some advanced reading material. You can leave a before-hours voicemail, or send a text if that's appropriate, but you want to be a day ahead. If the person has an administrative assistant, either confirm with that person (or at a minimum copy them in.)

Make it standard operating procedure. Whenever you set up a meeting or conference call, add a reminder in your calendar to check in the day prior to confirm the appointment. If you're traveling to see them, reach out the day before you leave.

Yes, the prospect gets another opportunity to cancel or reschedule. Something can always come up 24 hours before the meeting. And by confirming the meeting, you are granting them an out. It's a calculated risk, but it also telegraphs to them that you're organized and thorough, and that your time is valuable.

If a prospect needs to cancel a meeting, they're going to do it regardless whether or not you confirm it. There's little you can do to prevent a cancelation. But you can use this otherwise insignificant moment as another opportunity to qualify the account, reconfirm the meeting purpose, share an agenda, demonstrate your attention to detail and decrease the chance that your time is wasted.

All it takes is one cross-country, two-day trip for a meeting that gets canceled while you're standing in the customer's lobby to appreciate the value of a one-minute confirmation call. A cancellation can be informative, a way to advance the sales process, or a chance to show your sales skills. Or it can be an obligation.

The one thing it shouldn't be is a waste of time.

Getting Touches

Out of sight is out of mind. We live in a hyper-busy, hyper-distracted world (and as hard as it is to imagine, one that is becoming ever more so.) As salespeople, we're constantly competing for attention. In many instances, deals happen simply as a direct result of being able to stay front of mind with those making the decision.

This is especially true with complex or strategic deals where the sales cycle is protracted, the problem being solved is complicated, where something is already in place and 'working,' and/or you're competing for staff engagement, and/or integration resources and/or...well, you get the picture.

To use a sports analogy, you want to make sure you're getting meaningful 'touches' throughout the game. For example, any parent looking to develop their kid into a soccer prodigy knows that one of the most important factors is how much time they get on the field and with the ball. It's intuitively obvious, of course, but getting more touches early has huge implications for future success.

In the world of sales, the same rules apply. A complex and lengthy sales cycle may require you to 'touch' the customer fifteen or twenty or even fifty times to keep it moving, to maintain awareness and to elevate it to the priority it deserves. You don't want your project eclipsed by the sudden importance of other initiatives or distractions. And there are always distractions.

In most cases, you'll need to have touches with multiple people across an organization and throughout the sales process. It's a rare situation where any sizable deal is only influenced by one person. (And if you think you're in that situation, *that's* probably something you need look into.)

The challenge is in making the touches meaningful and frequent without being an inconvenience or intrusive. What's the right level of contact? What's the delicate balance where you're neither nonexistent nor irritant? How do you stay relevant and engaged, without turning into the stereotypical sales nuisance?

As with most answers to complicated questions, it depends. It varies by individual, with type and frequency of touch, by job title, the value of the touch to the customer and your level of established rapport.

Some of this gets easier with experience and gut feel (after 10,000 hours, for example), but there is as much risk in doing too little as in doing too much. You have a responsibility, after all, to fully represent and promote the value your company/product/service will deliver to the customer and so you need to make it a priority to them for the good of their enterprise. The trick is in how you do it.

As you look to connect with your customer over the arc of that big deal, there are a few things to keep in mind:

- **Brevity** – People appreciate details, but they appreciate even more a thoughtful summary that allows them to skim an important update. Provide the supporting material along with it, but as reference in case they want to drill down or forward it to a colleague.
- **Levity** – Not everything is serious. A little humor can take the edge off any interruption.
- **Value** – Few things scream desperation more than an empty email or a generic product pitch. Before sending anything, ask yourself if they would genuinely appreciate the interruption. (Remember, it's an interruption.)
- **On Target** – Make it specific. The more unique and targeted you can make that touch, the more effective it will be. Keep in mind that you're working with individuals with their own interests and idiosyncrasies.

A well-executed campaign of touches can make a huge

difference. Sometimes you're keeping the deal warm. Sometimes you're slowly identifying need. Sometimes you're educating them on some recent announcement, or industry news that should interest them, or getting them comfortable with some new idea, or with the company, or with you. In any event, you want to stay engaged.

You want touches.

Cards and Letters

It turns out that vinyl records aren't dead. In fact, they seem to be making a vigorous comeback. Want to guess what else isn't going away?

Paper. Paper consumption in the United States for the last twenty years has increased from 92 million tons to 208 million, a growth of 126%. (At the same time, The Washington Post recently reported that reading in the U.S, is at an all-time low, so thank you.)

My suggestion is that you embrace paper in at least one respect: Cards and letters. It's retro (which makes it very fashionable,) but it's also effective. For gifts, meeting follow up, passing along interesting articles or business cards from restaurants you think someone might like.

Sales Craft

This is my system. I have cards and envelopes printed with my name and address. (It's super classy.) They sit in a folder in my briefcase, complete with a book of stamps. If I see something of interest in a magazine, I'll tear it out and stuff it into an envelope with a quick note. "Saw this. Thought it interesting relative to your XYZ initiative." No product pitch, nothing remotely salesy.

Or right after a meeting, I'll scratch out a quick "I'm at a layover here at O'Hare Airport and wanted to quickly thank you for your time today…etc., etc."

Nobody does this anymore. And the disposable, ephemeral nature of email and texting make this sort of gesture stand out that much more. The physical arrival of a handwritten note in the mail is a genuine rarity. And another touch.

Q & A

Selling is just another form of problem-solving. The problem may be real, and it may be serious, like having software security exposure issues or needing more top-line revenue. Or perhaps the problem is trivial or imaginary, such as some slave to fashion *needing* that 20th pair of shoes. (I'm likely to get schooled by someone for describing shoes as *trivial*.) Whatever the reason, our job as salespeople is to solve problems.

To do that effectively, we first need to know what that problem is. But we need to know more. Things like:

- Does the customer recognize the problem?
- Are there other problems that need to be addressed?
- Is it a big enough problem that they want to overcome it?

- Do they define the problem the way that you do?
- Is the problem solvable? From whose vantage point?
- Who benefits from the solution? And who doesn't?

That's a lot to uncover, and in order to help solve this problem and make a successful sale we're going to need answers to questions like these. Some of this information can be gathered through background research and your own knowledge of the specific situation, but it all needs to be confirmed and substantiated with the customer. After all, the prospect may very well be contending with a serious security risk or desperately need to add customers and revenue, but unless they recognize that reality it's essentially impossible to solve the problem and complete the sale.

And to do that, we'll need to be able to ask questions and get meaningful answers.

The ability to effectively ask questions delivers several obvious benefits:

- It provides the chance to learn more about the customer – Both specifically about the issue(s) at hand, and more broadly.
- It conveys genuine curiosity and interest – It's natural to want someone to take an interest in us, right?
- It gives the customer the opportunity to contribute to and be engaged in the conversation – People generally appreciate an active, collaborative dialogue.
- It communicates your experience and understanding of the customer's business requirements – Done right, it's an opportunity to demonstrate expertise.

To do all this, we need an effective discovery strategy, one that relies on the ability to ask good questions and get revealing, useful information. This doesn't eliminate the need to construct and articulate an attractive solution, but every sales success begins by understanding the problem and making certain that the customer is seeing the same problem.

The challenge, of course, is getting answers to everything you need to know in a civilized, socially-acceptable way. It would be so much easier to simply hand the prospect a twenty-page questionnaire and wait for the results to come back, but that isn't happening.

A good discovery process requires strategy, tact and finesse. And time. Subject your client to a ham-fisted interrogation and they predictably shut down, become alienated, or worse.

What is your current discovery process? Examine it from every perspective. Consider the information you need to understand the problem, the client objectives, and the decision-making process. Budget, timing, key players, etc. are all obvious data points, but so are more esoteric (but equally important) details like "What happens to Bob Smith in Materials Sourcing when costs decline by 15%?" Or "How does the decision impact the folks in outside sales?" The goal here is to get a broader, more expansive perspective on the purchase impact, both positively and otherwise.

The process needs to be conversational. Nothing is as uniquely off-putting as a salesperson conducting a clichéd staccato-style, one-sided interrogation. You should be able to learn volumes about the company, customer, market and the big issues and do it in a relaxed, natural conversation.

Have a strategy - Part of the appeal of sales can be its unpredictability. It is by nature dynamic and complicated, usually with several major players and plenty of opportunity for mistakes, surprises and setbacks, so a tightly choreographed sales plan can only take you so far. Regardless, it pays off to identify what you don't yet know but should, the key data elements you'll need to gather and the general order in which you might approach collecting that information.

Have a list - You can download an editable Discovery Worksheet at www.brendanmcadams.com. That document has a core set of questions, and space to add questions specific to your circumstances, like 'Who is involved in the decision-making process?' And 'How does implementing this solution impact other departments?'

Again, it's a conversation and not a formal inquiry. Open questions that encourage dialogue are (usually) better. Who knows what you may learn if you simply allow your customer to ramble? There are times where simple yes/no questions are applicable, but they don't encourage the information-rich exchange that will help you find out what it is you don't know that you don't know.

Craft your questions – They should fit seamlessly into the dialogue. "What's your budget?" is essentially the same as "Given the economic conditions and the potential impact of the stimulus dollars that may come into play, what's your thinking around investment costs and expectation of returns?" Except that it's not. The first is abrupt and confrontational, while the second is thoughtful, informed, conveys interest in the prospect's thoughts and opinion, and is specific to the customer's requirements and circumstances. Plus, it's consultative.

Be curious - Not every question has to move you obviously forward. Genuine curiosity is disarming, and even flattering.

Take notes - You're uncovering a lot of important details, information that will require follow up and thought. Write it down. The client will likely appreciate the attention to detail and may even add to it as they see you taking note of something important. Especially any action items that you, or they, have committed to deliver on.

A critically important and powerful step at the close of any sales call is to summarize any follow up and action items that resulted from the conversation. The combined act of restating and writing it down reassures the client that you're committed to delivering on whatever promises were made during the conversation. Plus, it gives you a plausible reason to circle back and confirm what was understood.

It can be a smart strategy to ask a question to which you already know the answer in order to confirm an assumption, establish agreement, or challenge a position. There's no crime in being confused or needing more explanation. But be careful not to appear as though you haven't been listening. Like a baseball pitch, it's all in the delivery.

Sales Craft

Being skilled and creative in sales discovery is among the most important qualities a salesperson can develop, and one that is critical throughout the sales process. It's instrumental early in the sales cycle to understand customer needs and problems, but equally valuable later on to confirm assumptions and uncover changes in the selling situation. Whole sales books have been written on just developing the skills necessary to conduct an effective sales discovery process, and a thorough investment in this topic is worth every minute spent. Study up, practice, figure out what works and what doesn't, and hone this aspect of your craft.

Any questions?

Will You Just Listen?

Okay. You've asked the question. Now what?

Shut up and listen.

The stereotypical talking salesperson isn't a stereotype by accident. It's reality. Most salespeople simply talk too much.

Here's a better reality. Talk less. Listen more. Fight the urge to comment on everything or respond to every customer objection with some vivid, artfully crafted description of a product feature. We understand that it's not easy to fight off the urge to sell, but choosing to pick your battles and simply listen has advantages.

Here's why. Once the customer feels they can talk, and can

really explain something without interruption to a genuinely interested listener, the entire sales dynamic begins to change. You no longer have a customer across the table who feels they are competing to get a word in. Instead, they can take their time, relax, compose their thoughts, and speak at will. And given the opportunity, they invariably will.

Conversely, it's completely normal for a customer to shut down or provide terse, clipped answers to even complicated questions if they suspect you're not listening and are simply waiting for a pause in the conversation to counter with a product benefit or a knock on the competition.

Let them talk. Listen to what's being said *and* what isn't. What's important? What's bothering them? Where's the pressure coming from? Are things getting better, or worse? If you're doing it right, what you learn can be breathtaking.

Acknowledge without speaking. Nod. Smile. Show surprise. Or "Hmmm." Or "Really?" Then, when they've finished their point, wait. Take a second or two to see if they're actually done. The pause tells them that the floor is still theirs. You're interested. Go on.

Who knows where this may take you or what you might learn. They may go on to explain what the latest reorg means or who has a new project getting started. All you need to do is sit there and listen. Intently.

Yes, it might be about their maddening kids or last weekend's pool party. (They can't all be earth-shattering discoveries.)

Whatever may be said, it doesn't get said if you're busy talking.

Be aware of your body language. Are you leaning forward, or slouched? Where are you looking? Do you look interested? And when you do respond, pay attention to the tone of your voice and your delivery.

Be actively engaged, but relaxed. Don't interrupt. Let the customer completely finish her remark. Again, pause. It's brief, but apparent. It lets the customer know they can speak without interruption and at their pace. That you're listening. Often, they'll take right up again, sharing more and likely telling you, however indirectly, how to sell to them. If you're listening.

Listen for hard data *and* for softer emotional insights. Both are obviously important, and either might be good reason for further clarification and conversation. Who else in the organization is affected by whatever problem your solution will solve? Ask how they feel about the problem to further draw out the emotional significance.

Try not to dispute issues or argue every position. Let the client speak freely and at length. You can handle objections later. Often, simply being able to speak and be actively heard is enough to cause them to want to move forward. At a minimum, you've gained some goodwill.

If your competition is discussed during your meeting, it's best to avoid jumping in and disparaging them. It's inevitably safer to take the high road and focus on why your company or solution is the best choice. Or ask them to explain what it is that the competition is doing, what they like about them, or how they differentiate the various alternatives.

All of this is easier in a one-on-one setting. Add a third person and the sales call takes on a whole new dynamic. Bringing along a second salesperson adds even more complexity and is one reason why I prefer having more individual sales calls. (See page 133.)

With larger meetings, you'll need to be more rigorous with your 'listening strategy.' The internal prep call will mean discussing objectives and roles with your peer(s) before the call, potentially directing certain questions specifically to one or another and divvying up the conversation so that everyone feels they've had a chance to speak.

Done properly and with sales egos in check, a group sales call can take on a relaxed, conversational pace and be informative and effective. (Just don't expect the sorts of revelations that you can get speaking with someone one-on-one.)

Active, engaged listening takes effort, energy, skill and experience. And in my experience, the idea of active listening may be the most important lesson you can take from these pages. Once you get the hang of it and make it a habit, you can expect your client conversations to elevate to a completely different, more effective and professional level.

Become an expert at asking good, incisive questions. And then become an expert at listening intently and patiently. When you do, your customers will tell you how to sell to them, tell you how to beat the competition and tell you exactly how to win.

Just listen.

Sales Craft

Extras

Extras

Stretch. Raise your game. Add a new tool to your bag, and a new weapon to your arsenal.

Compressing Time

If you were to imagine the arc of a complex sales process, from the identification (or even better, the creation) of buyer interest to the point where a purchasing decision is finally made, there are any number of events (or client touches) along that arc where something happens.

There is a meeting, or some follow up, or a proposal, etc. There are mandatory events, like an initial client encounter or a purchasing decision (which might be to choose a competitor or not purchase at all.) There might be unanticipated events, such as a meeting cancellation or an objection. Or there could be other client touches intended to help position you or gather additional information.

Whatever those sales events happen to be, the sum of them delineate the many moments and events along that particular sales cycle. Some sales cycles have more events, others fewer. But the set of events for a given deal accomplished over time define that sales cycle.

Now imagine what would happen if you decreased the time it takes to get from start to finish for every sales opportunity over the course of a year by, say, 20%. How would that impact client satisfaction, your close rate, and ultimately your income?

A good sales executive does exactly that. He or she compresses time. It's not about eliminating steps or trying to take shortcuts. (In fact, a good salesperson will deftly add touches and events throughout the arc of the deal.) But it is about ways to make things happen more quickly, with less elapsed time. Simply put, your job is to compress that arc and shorten the time span between "Hello" and "Let's get started." Or otherwise, get more quickly to "No thank you." (See page 145.)

Despite the likely obviousness of this statement, it's rarely followed with the zeal and attention it warrants. Contrary to what you may have been told, good things don't come to those who wait. Time is your enemy. Time kills deals. Delay seldom works to a salesperson's advantage.

A fundamental tenet of your sales philosophy should be to continually find ways to shorten the time span between each step along the sales process. Think about how to respond at least a little bit faster than expected. Cut an hour, a day or even a week out of the time between stimulus and response, between when something is promised and when it's delivered. Every time you can shorten the time span between touches works to advance your deal to the next step and move things forward.

Compressing time as a fundamental sales practice accomplishes other objectives:

- It identifies you as responsive and effective,
- It gives your customer a sense of confidence in you as a business partner,
- And it can help to set the pace of the process, and thus forces your competitors to keep up. By keeping things moving, you're effectively positioning your competition as less responsive and less customer service-oriented.

This momentum works because an immediate B+ response is almost always better than an A- effort that doesn't happen until weeks later. And it stands to reason that you can craft a better response immediately, when it's still compelling and the details are fresh in your mind. (Besides, a thorough follow up reply, email or otherwise, can double as your sales notes.)

If necessary, send an early version of whatever deliverable you're working on stamped with DRAFT all over it, or with highlighted questions soliciting client feedback, drawing from your sales toolkit of prepared resources.

By adopting a commitment to compressing time, you gain the added advantage of staying sharp and in control. You've established an active, customer-centric momentum that helps propel the process forward. You're driving the sale rather than watching from the backseat.

Note that consistent efforts to compress time will often result in another client behavior. Customers certainly appreciate a timely response, but they can also start to expect it. So be prepared to sustain this practice. Getting things ahead of schedule, without having to ask or send reminders, allows your client to respond more quickly internally, look good with their peers, and generally appear to have their project(s) under control.

Admittedly, this tactic is simple (and obvious.) Respond quickly to emails, questions, or requests for additional information. Sales call follow up should be crisp and timely. Get the next step discussed and the next meeting scheduled as a normal course of the current conversation.

It's the mindset that requires effort. It demands that you make an attitudinal shift, adopting a sense of customer urgency that enables you to think about how you can compress time. Once your attitude is where it needs to be, you'll need to combine that with tools and processes to make time compression possible. (See page 49.)

Now, squeeze.

Admin Assistance

Early and frequent contact with key executive contacts is instrumental to any salesperson's immediate and long-term effectiveness. It is your best, most efficient chance to monitor the pulse of company objectives, organizational changes, and all the other inevitable and frustratingly unimaginative dysfunctions conspiring to ruin your year.

And who else is just as busy monitoring that pulse?

The administrative assistant. He or she (statistically speaking, executive office assistants tend to be female, so we're going with one pronoun here) is squarely situated at the confluence of rumor, reorg, purchasing and various other news streams. And more importantly, she manages your key executive's schedule, availability and attention span. Having her ear is a good path towards a closer relationship with her boss. So, you need to nurture that relationship.

Start by understanding that they aren't secretaries making copies and fetching coffee. A good executive assistant makes a sizable (if unappreciated) contribution to the company's accomplishments. And they can be invaluable to your success.

They're dialed into organizational changes, corporate edicts, and all sorts of valuable insights. I've had admins juggle appointments, hand me company directories, let me know exactly when their boss can take a five-minute call, tell me of upcoming birthdays, and give me the play-by-play on ridiculous office dramas. They'll email you org charts and explain why so-and-so in purchasing is a @#%!. And then they'll share advice on how to navigate around that person. You underestimate their influence at your peril.

Nurturing that relationship doesn't have to be difficult. Mostly, it's just common sense. For example:

- **Keep the admin informed** – Just like anyone, the admin wants to be viewed as smart, informed and capable. Make part of the conversation about the industry, about what's happening elsewhere in the company, or other detail.
- **Pass along news** – Use some important event or milestone as an opportunity to keep the executive informed, but do it through the admin. A short note or quick phone call explaining how "Sandy might find this of interest because…" has huge karmic value.

- **Solicit feedback and opinion** – "We're wrapping up our proposal and I wanted to ask you how..." or "What's going on over in marketing?" can be the catalyst for a priceless twenty-minute conversation on the company.
- **Be brief** – Ask for less time and let the admin be the miracle worker. Time is a valuable and misused commodity, so ask for thirty minutes (or ten) instead of an hour and let her show off her ability to juggle schedules. Then keep to it.
- **Make things easy** – The executive assistant is dealing with complex schedules and lots of loose ends, so come prepared with the solution. Make the job easier. Send along a draft agenda, email the appointment invitation, set up the conf call #, look up the driving directions to the restaurant or golf course, etc.
- **Be profuse with appreciation** – Quick follow up notes, updates and thank you's are mandatory follow up. Plus, you're front of mind it's time to ask for that executive's time and attention.

Invest in the administrative assistant and benefits accrue. You gain a valuable ally inside the company. You learn important details that will inform your strategy. And you get greater access to the executives that matter, when it matters.

In one especially notable instance, I had been trying to hastily arrange a presentation with several key prospects but couldn't get the calendars to sync up. The executive administrator, with whom I'd known for some time and with whom I thought I had a good relationship, seemed unable to find an hour that would work that wasn't over a month out. Given the one-on-

one communications I'd been having with the directors needed for the meeting, the delay was hard to understand.

Until the reorg, that is. It turned out that the administrator was slow-walking the process but couldn't tell me about the impending changes to the reporting structure. But her savvy saved me a bunch of wasted effort and the possibility of a lost deal.

Treat admins with the same respect, interest and preparation you would any other prospect. Talk to them rather than through them. Be respectful of their time. Be professional, but friendly. Smother them in thank you's. Treat them like the executive they report to, as though they are a key relationship in your overall sales strategy.

Because they are.

Companies ≠ Customers

Just as you wouldn't confuse your job with your career, don't confuse companies and customers. You might have a list of companies that make up your territory, but it is always the people at these companies that buy. Here's the simple math:

Companies ≠ People

Customers = People

Over the course of your rich and varied sales career, you will likely have the good fortune to meet and get to know an overwhelming number of prospects, partners and customers. Chances are that some of them will turn into great long-term friendships and hopefully most have the promise to become future working relationships. Regardless, they will inevitably bounce around among companies and industries over the years. They might get promoted or need a recommendation. Or they may go work for one of your competitors. Or perhaps provide you with a recommendation or a reference. Anything is possible.

It's easy to fixate on the company as 'the customer.' For most of us in sales, the company *is* the defining entity, part (or all) of one's sales territory, and ultimately the target, after all. It makes sense to equate someone in the company *as* the company, but it's not that simple. People get recruited, fired, move, get fed up and quit. Even a CEO, the face of the company, can go somewhere else. (Some of them can be odd, narcissistic and even sociopathic, but even sociopaths are people. Right?)

This also means that there's an excellent chance you'll run into these people throughout the arc of your career. Personally, I've been hired by past customers, and I've frequently been referred to other customers by past customers. I've even had a customer invest in my business.

In one memorable example, I found myself in the midst of an especially heated, contentious negotiation on what was one of the largest and most strategic deals of my career. I'd developed several solid relationships in the account, and in partnership with one fellow in particular had devised the framework for an exclusive customer/vendor affiliation. The proposed deal promised to dramatically increase our revenues, strategically position us with one of the largest health plans in the country and deal a significant blow to several competitors. All at once. And after a series of meetings, presentations and proposals, both sides agreed that this new, bigger relationship made sense and that a deal should be hammered out.

As the negotiations played out and we worked through the myriad details, my primary counterpart became increasingly adversarial and ultimately opposed to the deal terms. But the executive team above him wanted this done, and over the ensuing weeks he was sidelined unceremoniously from the negotiations. In the process, the friendly relationship we had established over the years became frayed and he ultimately left the company.

The story could easily end right there. Instead, we ran into each other awkwardly years later at an industry conference. Eventually, the conversation steered itself to that deal and our falling out. I ended up getting a much better perspective of the internal politics that he was enduring at the time and the implications of the deal. That chance interaction was the catalyst to reestablish our relationship, and he has since become one of my closest business friendships, something that would have been impossible to predict as I was consumed with one of the largest deals of my career.

In your daily sales efforts, keep in mind that your customers are people that go home to screaming kids and obligatory soccer games, have cats to feed, need to mow the lawn, have debts and ailing parents, and are hooked on Game of Thrones. So maybe it's not about you. Maybe it's the company culture that best explains their actions. Or something else entirely.

Sales Craft

And chances are they won't always be at that company.

When it comes to people, take the long view. Ultimately, it's not all business.

Sometimes it's personal.

Old Dogs & New Tricks

It's funny what you remember.

When I was a kid, one day my father brought home a set of cassette tapes. They were sort of a motivational program on creativity by a guy named Mike Vance. To give you some background, Vance's job was to energize and activate creativity at Walt Disney and, later on, at Apple. (Working for Walt and Steve. So...a pretty creative guy.)

I think I pretty much have the entire set of tapes memorized. Vance had all sorts of crazy ideas, recommendations to try, and 'out-of-the-box' thinking throughout. (Incidentally, he's the guy that popularized that term.) Listening to those six cassettes was like nothing I'd experienced before. It was transformative.

One particular anecdote had to do with the old saw that 'you can't teach an old dog a new trick.' Vance goes on to explain that that thinking is ridiculous. "Of course you can!" And why is that?

Because an old dog *appreciates* a new trick.

This is a fundamentally important idea. People love a new thing, whether it's the next gadget or shiny object or way to do something. They appreciate a new trick.

Be the dog that's always on the lookout for a new trick, a new way to do things, a better technique or tool. Not necessarily the next shiny object, of course, but it's hard to find gold if you don't pick up a few shiny objects along the journey.

For me, using video conference calling was one of those new tricks. (See page 107.) It came as a suggestion from a consultant that essentially insisted that our calls be conducted on Skype. Initially skeptical, I became convinced of the effectiveness of video when I realized how much less distracted my conversations were, and more memorable.

And with this whole internet thing right at your fingertips, you've no shortage of great ideas, troves of information, and innovative tools to discover, evaluate, and adopt (or not.) Maybe check out some of the many fantastic podcast options to pick up new ideas, listen to different opinions or simply stretch your brain. Or subscribe to a sales newsletter or two. (Or you might buy the occasional sales book, read it, and then buy copies for all your friends. It's just an idea...)

In short, make it a habit. Be on the hunt for that next transformative or liberating idea. The payoff is worth it. And these days, they are abundant and yours for the finding.

Because who doesn't appreciate a new trick?

Five Podcasts Worth Checking Out *

1. **'Exponential Wisdom'** Diamandis & Sullivan – For sheer out-of-the-box thinking

2. **'The James Altucher Show'** For some of the best interviews on the Internet

3. **'Accelerate! With Andy Paul'** Consistently good sales discussion.

4. **'Akimbo: A Podcast from Seth Godin'** Because everything he does is worth checking out.

5. **'The Gary Vee Audio Experience'** For sheer motivation and unbridled enthusiasm.

* Links available at www.brendanmcadams.com

Sales Presentations

Disaster may await, but (at least in my experience), it's incredibly rare that a roomful of people want to see your sales presentation fail miserably. They may be skeptical, they may prefer another vendor (or the status quo), or they may just want to get to lunch or back to their desk.

In reality, people seldom want to see you crash and burn. It may be a tough crowd, stern and silent, but they aren't wishing for disaster. Disaster is painful to watch. It's awkward and unpleasant. Plus, it makes time slow down and the meeting drag on. And nobody wants that.

So get that unproductive notion out of your head. Instead, consider this. They want you to win. Or at least not suck. For their own sake, if not yours.

Personally, I find the first three or four minutes the toughest. Get past that and things settle down. And as soon as someone asks a question or makes a comment, the whole mood of the meeting changes for me, so I actively solicit engagement early solely to help get me into my groove.

Figure out what works for you. Maybe it's sitting down at the conference table with the attendees (not always practical,) or standing protected behind a podium (not always available,) or you've got a proven introduction that you know by heart. Think about what gets you in your groove.

Whatever it is that gets you into that place, know that your audience is probably pulling for you to get there.

Conference Ambush

There are lots of little tips and tricks when it comes to attending conferences, but here's one that salespeople should do more often.

When attending conference presentations, make a point of being one of those people who go up and speak to the presenters afterwards. Say hello, mention some specific detail about why you enjoyed their talk, pose a thoughtful question or observation, and mention that you'll likely follow up with them later. You might ask for their card, but chances are their email was part of the presentation. Worst case, you can track it down later.

After the session is wrapped up is better than before the presentation unless you're very early and they're killing time.

Sales Craft

The panelist will likely be distracted with last minute details or chatting with the moderator. (But speaking with the keynote speakers in the main ballroom is tougher, and then you're looking more like an autograph hound than an interested colleague.)

Then follow up. You'll need to let them get settled back in the office, so a couple days may need to pass. Then send an email. Remind them of the conversation. Maybe a LinkedIn invite. (Maybe?)

See where it goes.

Lobby Ambush

Truthfully, I wouldn't believe this was still a thing if I didn't recently witness it directly. Here's how it goes…

It's the end of the quarter and your customer still hasn't signed off on the deal, so senior management commands the salesperson to fly to said customer's city and park themselves in the company lobby with the explanation that they are there until the deal gets closed. (It's evidently best to arrive a day or two prior to quarter end.)

Except that this can't possibly work anymore, can it? It didn't in the examples I witnessed.

If you're in the situation where the sale hinges on harassment tactics like this, there are too many other problems with the

Sales Craft

deal, with your sales skills, or with the customer. (Not to mention sales management.)

And those problems can't be solved by parking your ass in the lobby and waiting them out.*

Enough said.

---

* If you have stories to the contrary, please email me at brendan@brendanmcadams.com. I have to hear them.

The Big Meeting

Your CEO and other senior executives can be among the most effective sales tools in your arsenal. The operative words here: *Can be*. Think of them like cruise missiles. Very effective when judiciously deployed. Otherwise, you could be inviting disaster.

Key takeaway - Making sure it's not a disaster is entirely your responsibility.

But stay with me, because having the right senior executive in the right sales situation is a truly beautiful thing to behold. Your customer relaxes and opens up, the conversation is elevated and expansive, new opportunities unfold before your eyes, and your sales credibility is exponentially enhanced. So you want to use this tactic. You just want to be sure you don't

101

screw it up because there's no place to hide if everything blows up.

Perhaps the best opportunity to leverage your C-level resources is in the big meeting. The big meeting probably needs no additional explanation, but the basic ingredients are:

- Senior executives from both companies,
- A compelling event, and
- You're in the room.

There are things you can do to make sure nothing explodes. Rigorous preparation is key, which requires you to pay attention to the following:

- **Handle the details** - This means setting up the meeting, confirming attendees, drafting and vetting the agenda, coordinating lunch, whatever.

- **Manage the message** - It's your account, so you should help determine the agenda. What needs to be accomplished? Who needs to say what? What issues might the customer bring up? Are there specific supporting documents?

- **Act as Master of Ceremonies** - You're not the senior person in the meeting, but you should nonetheless play a role. That includes introductions, coverage of relationship history, current status, small talk that gets the conversation going. Most importantly, you need to deftly keep the meeting on track. Which means making sure you're hitting the key meeting objectives outlined above.

- **Follow up** - The best part of a successful big meeting is the follow up. Own it. That doesn't mean you have to solve the big hairy product problem or draft the legal language for an expanded partnership, but it does mean you're making sure it gets done, and in a timely fashion. And the corollary is that it's not the responsibility of your senior executive. Take that off their plate and assume the sales leadership role you're supposed to be playing.

- **Communicate** - Work your follow up list and keep everyone apprised of the progress being made and the accomplishments achieved, as well as any sticking points or obstacles. Be judicious and practical about what warrants escalation, but it's the post-meeting activity that keep the momentum and dialogue going.

Of course, your senior executive needs to be the right fit and they need to be up to the task. Discreetly ask around to see what sort of experiences other salespeople have had, what the executive likes and doesn't like, or any idiosyncrasies that you need to factor in. This is a big wager with outsized egos and personalities, so the potential for unintended consequences is significant.

But hey, why not roll the dice? Some of my favorite meetings were completely unpredictable and totally off-script. But they were exciting, successful rides all the same. One particular CEO could keep you waiting an hour or more, then show up in shorts and Hawaiian shirt, and then simultaneously eat and talk for the next two hours of a scheduled one-hour time slot. But the conversations, wherever they happened to go, (and they could go anywhere,) were always brilliant and riveting, leaving the client awed and convinced that this was the company to bet on.

The big meeting with the senior executive has its inherent risks, but the payoff can be worth it. Just keep things from backfiring and you'll be fine.

What's Plan B?

What could possibly go wrong? The self-help, positive-thinking crowd would suggest that you should always focus on the ideal outcome, force all negative thoughts from your being and imagine total, limitless success. Which is fine, up to a point.

But another way to think about things is to step up and ask yourself, "What can go wrong?" Sure, your solution is the best option for the customer. Yes, the client has all but signed. Still, in that moment, take some time and try to imagine all the ways your deal could go sideways.

This isn't a prescription for worry or a suggestion that you're being too easy on yourself. Rather, taking time to imagine disaster has the curious effect of making it less likely.

Think about applying this tactic at the various stages of every deal. Make it part of your standard practice. Ask yourself what could go wrong. Where are the problems, weaknesses and unknowns? How could you lose the deal? Who is against you? What needs to happen for disaster to strike?

Use NASA as an example. There's arguably no more skeptical, worrisome, hand-wringing crowd on the planet. They spend tens of thousands of hours trying to anticipate all the disastrous, life-threatening events that could befall any project. Most of them never come to pass. Fewer still don't have a solution already in place.

Salespeople seldom formalize this 'imagine a deal-breaking calamity' component of the sales process. The result is, there's no Plan B when a calamity does strike. There's no deft recovery because nobody could imagine the need for one. Until there is.

The interesting aspect of the NASA philosophy regarding serious problems is that they're made less serious simply because they've already planned for them. By anticipating the problem, they've given themselves the time to resolve it beforehand. It's not even really a surprise. It's just another step, another plan that needs to be executed.

Make a habit of asking what can go wrong before it does, and then having a Plan B becomes second nature.

You won't need it. Probably.

In Front of the Camera

Here's a quick tip. Whenever practical, turn your scheduled conference calls and demos into video calls. The advantages are innumerable, but here are a few:

- **Engagement** – You see them. They see you. Which means they have to pay attention, and it means *you* have to pay attention. You can't check email or surf the web (or shouldn't), which means you're getting more of them. And they're getting more of you.

- **Information** – Video delivers a better, more complete and nuanced interaction. You're seeing facial expressions, boredom and excitement, distraction and the interpersonal activity of those on the other end of the camera.

- **Novelty** – Video is still underutilized, so using it is a differentiator. If properly executed.

- **Impression** – Done well, it provides you another chance to make a professional impact and convey competence.

These days, conducting a video call takes little more that activating the camera on your computer and hitting a button on the web conference application. But do it right. Wear a professional outfit. (Business casual is usually fine, but no ratty t-shirts or PJs.) And make sure your office environment conveys the right message.

Start by practicing with your internal team or partners before you start in on your customers. But start. It's too easy and too effective not to.

Keep in Touch

This is particularly for the remote sales professional. If you're not in the main office, chances are you work from home. You've cordoned off a room or the attic or wherever, and that's where you ply your trade. (Mine's in the basement now, and formally referred to as The Nerve Center.)

In this environment, it's easy to hunker down and work away for hours at a time. You can settle in wearing your ratty t-shirt or pajamas and only extract yourself long enough to eat and use the facilities. But you shouldn't. As a remote employee or freelance salesperson, you need to mingle.

Make mingling a habit. Find time for regular communication with others in the company. It's easy to be 'out of sight, out of mind' when you're out in the field, so let those back in HQ know what you're doing and how you're fighting the good fight.

Give yourself a reminder to call other team members regularly just to see what they're hearing, share anecdotes about what works, or what you've learned about a competitor, etc. Emails and texts are okay, but they're not enough. People need to hear a voice and see a face. A disembodied text message isn't the same thing.

And find other ways to stay engaged. I've never been a college basketball fan and so the whole March Madness thing doesn't resonate much with me, but I still do the brackets and try to 'keep it real' with the corresponding trash talk. (Bonus tip: Just pick teams randomly based on how much you like the uniform colors or the mascot. That strategy has worked perfectly for me, ensuring that I'm never burdened with the hassle of collecting the winnings.)

When you're out in the field, it's easy to be invisible. Stay in touch.

Sell by Walking Around

One of the seminal business books of the 1980's, *In Search of Excellence* by Tom Peters and Robert Waterman, (kudos to you if you're too young to know of it) explained the importance of 'managing by walking around.'

The idea was that you learned things, absorbed the culture, uncovered problems and opportunities, and understood how things worked within your organization most effectively by being on the ground and among your team. Maybe this is obvious now, but it was then for many readers one of the bigger takeaways from the book.

Back in the early days of my sales career, I picked up on a variation of this approach from a Sun Microsystems sales guy.

We both shared territory at AT&T and specifically Bell Labs. While I was selling them database software, Ed was busy setting them up with literally hundreds (or maybe even thousands?) of Sun servers.

One ingredient fundamental to his success was his vendor badge. By having a vendor badge, Ed could enter the building at will and roam the halls of various Bell Labs facilities with impunity. He'd poke his head into offices and cubicles, ask about projects, hand out literature and tchotchkes, and basically act like a fellow employee.

And for all practical purposes, he was. It was brilliant and transformative. He was part of the AT&T fabric and knew about projects and reorganizations long before I did. He was on top of technical issues before they blew up. He could track down and meet with engineers in real-time. This was an epiphany for me, and I immediately set to work finding a client to sponsor my own vendor badge. (A significant part of my pitch was that they'd no longer have to walk down to the main entrance to sign me in.)

Later, when I was responsible for selling to Citigroup, I was able to secure a vendor badge that gave me similar access. I'd arrive at the main IT offices early and have my coffee in the company cafeteria on most mornings. Parked there afforded me the opportunity to informally catch up with various people (especially the hard to reach executives) in an environment that lent itself to more casual, collaborative conversations. I'd become a familiar fixture, ultimately converted from being some outside vendor to part of the team.

Since Sept. 11th, it isn't as easy to get customers to advocate a vendor badge, nor is corporate security as likely to grant it. But the idea of selling by walking around remains worth pursuing.

Be on the lookout for opportunities to walk freely among your customers.

Five Things Not to Order at a Customer Lunch

1. Spaghetti

2. A (second) martini

3. Breakfast

4. A prune smoothie

5. Chocolate cake

You Gotta Eat

Get in the habit of frequenting a few good restaurants near your clients' offices. Get to know the staff *and* the manager. Make a point of recognizing their effort, in both word and deed. Finally, let them know you're planning to be a regular.

You don't need to make a big deal out of it. There's no need to show off, but having the restaurant looking out for you a little more than the average visitor makes a difference. Maybe you arrange to have an appetizer arrive just after you're seated. Or the chef "throws together something he thought you'd like."

This dining strategy gives you the ability to recommend entrees, know the wine list (and which expense-busting vintages to avoid,) and focus your attention on your guests rather than the menu.

And you definitely want to have the waiter run your credit card beforehand, so the bill never makes it to the table. As unlikely as it may be, this eliminates any possibility of a confrontation about who picks up the check.

These are little things. They're just details, but that's where the Devil is.

Who is Your Coach?

Big, complicated, strategic deals are invariably fraught with a maelstrom of people, issues, requirements and motivations. Companies seldom function with the silky-smooth precision of a Swiss watch. More often, you're dealing with a hotbed of internal conflict, dysfunctional management, or simply an inability to execute. Getting a successful outcome and a closed deal requires you to effectively uncover, anticipate and address all these obstacles. And more.

Doing that without help is tough under the best of circumstances, and in a large organization with lots of players and complex office politics it can be impossible. You've got limited time, visibility and access. Even in situations where the salesperson is dedicated to one account, there's only so much one can see and learn as an outsider.

You Need A Coach
By definition, a coach is someone in the client organization who can advocate for you and/or provide you with insider insights that can improve your odds of winning. They can read the tea leaves, tell you how your presentation landed with the key people, review documents before you send them to their bosses and help in countless other ways.

Having a sales coach isn't a new idea, and I credit the Miller-Heiman folks for bringing the concept to life for me years ago. Basically, the goal is to have key people inside the company that can actively assist in your sales efforts. Typically (but not always,) your coach is involved in the deal, is looking for a certain decision, and has goals closely aligned with your own.

Simply put, your coach wins when you do. They have a certain, specific corporate outcome they're looking to accomplish, and your solution helps them to advance that outcome. Your success is their success, and they're savvy enough to know that helping you behind the scenes is good career and business strategy.

A Coaching Session
Perhaps the best example I can point to happened entirely by accident. I was deep into a strategic deal to be the data warehousing standard for a large Wall Street firm. Part of my preparation process is to work through the sales strategy on big sheets of paper. I would scribble out the various details of the deal: key buying criteria; decisionmakers, influencers, advocates, users; timelines; action items; etc. Each section of the worksheet would have items added and others crossed out.

Each worksheet was a living document and my physical, paper-based CRM.

Placed purposely in the center of the worksheet was the most critical element to my sales strategy, the client's organization chart. Drawn by hand, with hierarchies scribbled in and scratched out, it was rich with detail, check marks and notes alongside various names. It was also a mess, but one that I could interpret in a glance. It was my sales roadmap. Each important deal would have a similarly chaotic-looking but information-rich roadmap, the one source of truth that would go with me everywhere.

On a flight to Denver, I was seated in first class with one of my key clients for the deal. He had his nose buried in a book, so I quietly pulled out the sales worksheet for our deal, figuring I could use the time to do some last-minute preparation prior to the upcoming dinner meeting.

After a few minutes, my customer looked up from his book, curious about what I was working on. "Just reviewing notes before dinner," I explained. My terse response didn't satisfy his curiosity, which was now locked onto the worksheet (and the organization chart in particular), which he then pulled from my grasp and inspected thoroughly, muttering "Huh, interesting."

An awkward silence followed. We were now months into the sales cycle for this particular deal and the worksheet reflected it. It was heavy with notes, comments and observations on all the key players. Including the guy now scrutinizing it.

After a minute, he said "No, this isn't right." He then took my pen, flattened the page out on the airplane tray table, and began to edit my org chart. He added names and titles, simultaneously explaining what each correction and whether they were for or against the project and why. Stunned by the experience playing out, I scrambled to keep up and remember everything he was saying.

This coaching session continued for several minutes. He explained in specific detail the need for a new database platform, the reasons why our solution was better, who had a vested interest in the competition and why, and what I needed to watch out for. It was a sales epiphany.

To that point, we had what I'd consider a good relationship - professional and collaborative, but with reservations. Suddenly, we were at a completely different level. The conversation had changed, and he was now explaining details that were sensitive and even confidential, priceless information that would put him at some risk were it to get out.

What changed? Clearly, it was my dog-eared sales worksheet. With that document, he knew that I was serious and prepared. There were gaps and errors in the worksheet, of course, but he figured I had a coherent strategy, which meant that I could be trusted, was worth betting on and investing in. In short, we could be a team.

And from that moment onward, we were a team. He would tell me who needed more convincing, what the key messages were for which audience, who was still on the fence and whether they mattered. Maybe I could have won the deal without him (unlikely), but together we were unstoppable.

You need a coach. (And maybe more than one.) Someone to point out the blind spots, break down the competition, and elevate your game.

Finding Your Coach

To find your coach, you'll need to figure out who wants you to win, (or who *should*.) And generally speaking, the higher up the food chain, the better.

Once you have that person (or persons) identified, it's as much art as science, but it's all selling. At a minimum, you'll need to clearly demonstrate:

- **Competence** – Your client needs to be confident that you know what you're doing, that you understand the problem, the solution, and how to sell professionally. Without this, you can't accomplish the next step.

- **Trust** – The client needs to know that you're reliable, that he or she can count on you, that you get stuff done. They cannot afford to hang their career on someone that can't execute, that might embarrass them, or worse.

- **Influence** – Your client has to believe that you have credibility and influence inside your company. Do you have the CEO's ear, can you rally resources, will you be able to get things fixed when there is a serious problem?

- **Composure** – Are you unflappable, presentable, executive material? Do you make the client look good? Will you stay cool when things aren't?

It's not easy to pull this off, and you may not be able to establish a bona fide coach for every deal. Customers are understandably wary, and it's easy to get burned by some slick sales guy. But earn that kind of working relationship and you can expect your whole perspective on professional sales to change.

Along with your win percentage.

YES. And NO.

Saying YES feels so good. You're being agreeable. It's polite and accommodating. You're satisfying the client requirements and thus, ipso facto, moving the deal closer to a win.

You can't help it. You want to agree. You want them to be happy. And doesn't saying YES seem like it will make your client a little happier?

YES is positive, and implies a certain momentum to it. It's inherently optimistic.

NO, on the other hand, just sits there, imposing and stubborn and negative.

But to be a bona fide professional salesperson, you need to be able to say NO.

It's not exclusively the right of customers to disagree or refuse. When asked, you need to be able to state clearly that the product doesn't do something if it doesn't do that thing. Or that it will cost (a lot) more to customize it so that it *can* do that thing. Or that they really shouldn't want the product to do that thing, and here's why.

Salespeople need to be able to say NO to incessant hoop-jumping, that thing where a prospective client makes ridiculous, pointless requests simply because they think they can. Because they've come to the conclusion, mistakenly, that salespeople can just be told what to do.

And you must be able to *really* say NO to a bad deal or a bad customer. When confronted, sale professional can say NO:

- When the product doesn't do what they ask.

- When the customer lies or makes an inappropriate request.

- When the deal has no profit margin and none in the future. There are customers out there that refuse to recognize your need to generate a reasonable margin. Let your competitors deal with those customers.

- When the customer is ill-suited to your offering. (Hard to walk from, but you know it's right.)

- When you know the customer is destined to become a support nightmare.

The thing about saying NO is that it gets easier to say once you've done it a few times. Your clients aren't accustomed to hearing it from their vendor, so it might take them by surprise. But it's another little thing that will differentiate you from the sales 'talent' they're used to dealing with.

Done right, a well-intended NO will result in you hearing a lot more of YES when it matters.

Five Gadgets from the Sales Archives*

1. Palm Pilot

2. RIM Blackberry Curve

3. Motorola StarTac flip phone

4. Motorola Bravo pager

5. Compaq Portable II computer (with Lotus 1-2-3)

* And there's a story for every one of them.

Making Introductions

Here's a quick tip. Make a habit of introducing your customers to each other.

This is only my opinion, but part of your job is (or should be) to connect people and help foster relationships. Doing so further differentiates you by emphasizing your role, not as someone trying to make the next sale, but as a trusted advisor and colleague.

When you get your customers talking to each other about you and your company, you've got no choice but to stay on your toes and do your job. When you actively encourage and even invite that interaction, you're making it clear you're confident and have nothing to hide.

More importantly, consider the value it provides to your customers. These are introductions not otherwise likely to be made, for competitive reasons or due to geographic separation. But the benefit can be great, whether for career advice or sharing perspectives about the industry. Or just networking. And you will have made that relationship happen.

I've made more customer-customer introductions than I can count, and always to good effect. The initial logic was to help my sales efforts, figuring that a prospective customer is more likely to believe my customer's favorable reference than they are me. And while it tends to be a 'warts and all' assessment, it has consistently proved a sound strategy.

It's typically initiated during a meeting or phone call, as in "You need to talk to this guy. His application does exactly what you're talking about." Or it could be as simple as providing an unsolicited reference scrawled onto a business card, with a follow up email to both contacts.

One inevitable outcome of these connections is the personal razzing I receive, with my particular idiosyncrasies and character flaws explicated in painful detail. (I guess it's a small price to pay.)

So, from time to time, give some thought to picking up the phone and telling someone, "Hey, you should meet…"

An RFP... Now What?

I think there have been four unsolicited Requests for Proposal (RFP) wins in the course of my sales career. *Four.* That's an average of one every... never mind. Of course, that may suggest that I suck at RFPs. Or it may mean that the deal was skewed to the favor of some other vendor. (I'm going with the second one.)

Here's my advice. Apply serious scrutiny to an unsolicited RFP. Unless you're dialed in to win the deal because you helped design it or have some huge competitive advantage, the unsolicited RFP is almost always a genuine time sink at a minimum or, worse, a chance to spill all sorts of confidential information that could easily end up with the winning vendor. In my experience, it's rare to win an unsolicited RFP. Conversely, I think I've won essentially every RFP that I knew of and/or helped craft from the start.

It's easy for me to tell you to pass on a deal, and probably just as difficult for you to heed that advice. But experience tells me that you're better off picking up the phone and making a cold call (or taking the day off and playing golf) than investing huge hours, energy, enthusiasm and your karma in longshots.

It's also difficult to explain to sales management that you should skip this one. It's not natural for salespeople to walk away from a deal (although there are plenty of instances where they should.) This is especially true when the request comes to you thirty pages thick, asking for prices and promising the beginning of a long and beautiful relationship. Alas, that beautiful relationship is probably with the vendor that helped them write the RFP.

This is a lesson I was fortunate to learn early in my sales career. We were responding to an RFP for a new initiative that AT&T was looking to launch in a matter of a few months, and the opportunity promised to be *enormous*. My company had been invited because we had a reputation for being good at large-scale, systems integration efforts. Beyond those capabilities, we didn't have any particular competitive advantages that we could emphasize. But we responded because at this particular company "That's what we do."

We proceeded to amass a team to develop the response, answer all the questions, prepare an extensive budget and get it all packaged up for delivery. The final deliverable was beautiful, formatted and bound, and as professional as a proposal could be.

But I didn't have a good feeling about it. Our costs seemed ridiculously high and our execution times long relative to what I would have expected, or what the prospect had outlined. Regardless, as the salesperson of record I dutifully submitted it a couple hours prior to the deadline.

It was the next day when I got the call from the customer, who it turned out was an outside consultant tasked with the vendor evaluation process. There was a noticeable distress in her voice as she asked me about our response. I answered her questions over the next couple of minutes, during which she seemed to relax. I then asked what was concern exactly, to which she replied with surprising candor. "Your response was four times higher than the next highest vendor response, and we were worried that we had missed an important step in our rollout strategy."

Nope. They hadn't. We just weren't a good fit.

When you get that unsolicited RFP, figure out if you're a real fit. Maybe you need to respond, even when you know it's wired for the other competitor. Sometimes it makes sense to do so if only to help the customer bulk up the responses or as an opportunity to make this prospect aware of all your capabilities.

In the latter case, it's often an infinitely better strategy to redefine the response and solution in such a way that it forces the customer to think differently about the problem. They ask for A, B and C, but you come back with a custom proposal and solution that puts your offering in the best possible light.

This approach should require less time and resources for you and your team because you're drawing from existing internal resources and don't have to adhere to their proposal format. You still look thoughtful and responsive, and perhaps provided some valuable consulting. Just maybe your renegade proposal causes them to rethink the project scope and/or scuttle the RFP process, prompting the client to ask you to come in under new circumstances to talk.

The unsolicited, surprise RFP (or its close cousin, the Request for Information) is usually a low probability shot. It's a Hail Mary. And as much as we love watching that big hopeful but desperate pass into the end zone, it seldom ends in a touchdown.

And it's not a strategy.

Smaller Calls

More is better. But smaller can be better, too.

We're talking about sales calls, of course. The most effective, informative conversations are one-on-one. The same is true with sales calls. How often have you ever experienced a truly productive, interactive session when there are even five or six people? The group dynamic becomes too powerful, and it only gets worse as more people get added to the mix.

Ideal sales calls are engaged, active conversations. The goal is to learn, understand, educate, connect, influence and motivate. With every added contributor, you're also adding complexity and the problems inherent with that dynamic. Whenever possible, make your sales call smaller, with fewer participants.

More people also means more choreography and planning, so think carefully about who to include and specifically what role each attendee should play. A more complex chemistry is at work here. Who talks? What needs to get accomplished? Who leads? Orchestrating a meaningful, productive conversation among even a handful of people can be challenging, and it's the rare team that pulls it off effectively. Personalities and egos are inevitable, creating a situation that's difficult enough to navigate with your customer, let alone among your internal team.

Simple math also plays a role. Adding someone from your team to the meeting potentially subtracts from the time that the customer can speak. Perhaps significantly. That rarely leads to a good outcome. You want your customer to feel free to speak openly and at length, but every additional attendee works to eat into that possibility.

Ask yourself if a particular person is critical to the conversation. Can they help move things forward, build credibility, drive discovery or solution definition? If yes, then include them. Otherwise, they're complicating the process, putting an added barrier between you and your customer, and decreasing the likelihood of a productive meeting.

Of course, some situations prevent you from disinviting attendees. This is less a problem with customer attendees (unless they're at risk to share sensitive information with your competitor or disrupt the conversation) than with your fellow employees. In these instances, who attends will likely require some negotiation.

For your teammates that do attend, you need to clearly convey your meeting objectives during the sales prep session. Even something as simple as explaining that "during the first twenty minutes I want to learn about X and Y, and that I want to leave ten minutes at the end to talk about our support plan" can help your team appreciate that you have a strategy, and that they're a part of it.

If you can also explain *what* they should plan to contribute (and discuss what those comments might be), that guidance can have a significant impact on your meeting's effectiveness. Importantly, detailing these roles and expectations helps to reinforce to the team that you're leading the meeting and have a specific objective in mind.

When you can, consider breaking the meeting up. It's almost always better to have three one-on-one conversations than one large session. (The obvious exception might be in the case of conducting a demo or a more formal presentation.)

A group engagement can be advantageous, but not always. People are more open when they are not competing with their peers for talk time, and they'll often share specifics they would never volunteer in a group setting. The group presentation *can* prove invaluable to understand the political dynamic you're contending with, but one-on-one conversations are a better avenue to establishing rapport and getting candid feedback.

Ultimately, touches and meaningful interactions are more effective in small settings. Invest in small calls. They lead to bigger things.

The Mental Game

The Mental Game

Time for some philosophy. Let's think about the thought process. Consider sales strategy and ponder the Big Picture. If this really is your calling, it warrants some contemplation.

Credit is Overrated

Let's make a bold prediction. Your sales success is inevitable.

Of course, there will be setbacks and obstacles along the journey. Losses and low points. Huge quotas and 'problematic' product offerings. Bad bosses and lousy territory assignments. You'll have moments when you doubt your abilities and wonder if your decision to pursue a career in sales was the right one. We've all been there. It comes with the territory. (I had a regional sales manager throw a phone at me once. Seriously.)

But you'll also have plenty of great meetings and presentations, successful negotiations and fantastic follow up. You'll win deals and earn new customer relationships. They'll pile up, a testament to your abilities and your dedication. Again, it's inevitable.

When that happens, let others take the credit. Better still, be proactive and effusive with detailed accounts of how your teammates stepped up. Make sure that others, and especially the team that helped bring it in, get the recognition and attention. Advertise their contributions, praise them in public settings and remind senior management of their efforts. Be specific and memorable. "Tony spent countless hours, stayed late all last week to get the Winklebinder file out" or "Have you seen the new demo that Linda put together for InterTechnoCorp? It's amazing!"

The thing about credit and recognition is that they have a remarkable shelf life when bestowed on others, but go stale almost immediately when self-directed. Imagine soccer great David Beckham celebrating a corner kick goal. Regardless how stunning the achievement, he has seconds to run around in jubilation before it becomes unseemly. Within moments, his coach will have returned to a 'What can you do for me now?' attitude. And so should Beckham.

And while your own accomplishments may be Beckham-caliber, the self-congratulatory pronouncements had better be similarly short-lived. But weeks later you can very confidently gush that "Sarah here saved our ass on the StratoComm demo last month! We couldn't have won it without her."

Victory is intoxicating, certainly. It's thrilling to relive the Herculean effort and brilliant execution that you put together to bring in the big win. That's what selling is about, at least as much as the money. Savor your wins. Appreciate them, of course, and quietly celebrate them.

But credit is a by-product best spread generously around. You don't need to be quiet about that.

Five Things to Bring to Every Industry Conference

1. Comfortable shoes

2. Business cards

3. An extra business outfit. And jeans.

4. Pre-printed FedEx or UPS airbills and packing tape

5. A good book (See page 154.)

Killing Your Deal

A critical skill for any sales professional is the ability to determine a genuine, qualified sales opportunity from a time sinkhole. Few things are better at derailing a salesperson's productivity, reputation, compensation and morale than truly fruitless sales efforts. This isn't about deals above your ability or tough competitive slogs, but specifically about opportunities that won't close because there isn't a reason to buy, they can't or won't make a decision, or they simply aren't buying from you. Your job is to be able to identify a genuine, qualified sales opportunity and differentiate it from those that aren't.

But how? The best way to figure out if you've got a deal is this: Try to kill it.

To be specific here, this is not to say you should let your efforts slide, neglect your client, or otherwise practice shoddy sales efforts. And we're not suggesting that you under- or misrepresent your product/service offering. You still have to deliver 100% throughout the process. Suit up, present your ass off, be your reliably charming self 24 x 7. But part of your showing up requires you to actively challenge your customer to prove that they want and can buy what you're offering. There is a point, and in a long sales cycle there may be multiple points, where you need the prospect to convince *you* that they can become a viable, genuine customer.

It's 'trying to kill the deal' because you're actively scrutinizing whether it is a viable opportunity *for you*. This is a serious examination of the sales opportunity from the perspective that the potential doesn't justify the effort. Is this deal worth your company's time and effort? And is it worth yours?

Here's the kicker. To do this, you'll need to engage the customer.

How exactly? Essentially, the customer needs to actively justify their motivation to purchase what you offer. They need to confirm their purchasing intentions and convince you that they're serious. You're asking them to make a business case for moving forward.

I was working on a high-profile data warehousing opportunity with a large financial institution, a strategic deal that meant millions in future revenue. And while we had a good technical story and could win in theory, we were the clear underdog to the incumbent, approved-vendor alternative. The sales process had been unusually demanding, with multiple technical presentations, reference calls, and executive meetings. And to that point in the sales cycle, the customer hadn't made any indication that we had a legitimate shot.

The client then announced that they wanted us to coordinate a site visit with a specific, similarly high-profile customer of ours. The requested visit meant a significant investment for my company, juggling multiple schedules, getting cooperation from our customer (who had to suffer through too many such interruptions already), flights and hotels for several staff. It even required hosting the prospective customer's team for a dinner the evening prior to the on-site session.

To that point, we had no idea if we were winning or losing and every reason to believe that the deck was stacked against us.

Facing valid internal concern that this wasn't a deal worth chasing, it became clear that we needed some indication that we were being taken seriously. If not, we needed to back away and accept our losses.

The person who could definitively answer this burning question, and the key decisionmaker for this deal, was a director who'd been instrumental in selecting the incumbent vendor. Gruff, respected and hard to pin down, he was the guy we needed to talk to.

On the premise that we had to discuss details of our upcoming site visit, I was able to arrange a brief one-on-one meeting.

After some formalities, I wound up my resolve, enumerated the various steps we were taking and the scrutiny being placed on me to win this deal, and reminded him that he was the company's executive sponsor to our primary competitor. Then I asked "Respectfully, do we have a legitimate shot here? We're making a significant investment here and I need to be able to reassure my executives that we aren't chasing our tails."

The question seemed to amuse him. He smiled, leaned back in his chair, and said "Honestly, it's yours to lose." Almost like a criminal that, finally caught, feels compelled to share every detail of their crime, he then proceeded to explain the situation and the ensuing sales process. That his current vendor had become complacent, that our technology impressed him, that for political reasons he needed to be particularly rigorous in bringing another database technology to support.

Ultimately, we did win the deal as he predicted (or pronounced.) But why did the meeting succeed? Three reasons. First, timing. We had by that point invested enough effort and energy to prove we were a serious option. To have asked the same question early in the process would have shown impatience and arrogance. Second, that it was a one-on-one meeting meant no witnesses. He could keep to his plan knowing that anything I might repeat would be discounted as some rookie sales guy's optimism. And third, the question was direct and even confrontational, an approach that any self-respecting Wall Street executive would appreciate.

Hopefully, the value of this tactic, however frightening it may seem, is self-evident. Done correctly, you end up knowing with much greater certainty that there is a deal, how to properly forecast it and what level of investment you should make to achieve the win. But the customer gains in equal measure because if it's a real deal, they should be able to expect better support and access to resources throughout the sales process. Plus, they gain a vendor with better insight into their problems and objectives, one better prepared to craft a tailored and more effective solution.

How you manage this is the challenge, and a lot of it has to do with experience and confidence. After all, nobody wants to intentionally sabotage a perfectly good sales opportunity.

As intimated above, your ability to employ this approach is somewhat dependent on style and geography. In my experience, you can be more direct and even confrontational on Wall Street than on Main Street. In other cases, perhaps the easiest technique to adopt is a Columbo-esque (a 70's era TV detective) confusion that starts with something like "This doesn't seem like the right time for you/your company to take this initiative on." Or "Is your organization really in need of this level of product/investment?"

You can be even more specific, stating something like "This project seems fraught with all sorts of political/financial/ implementation challenges. Is everyone bought in?" Let the prospect explain their reasoning for the deal (if there is one) and leverage your curiosity and 'confusion' with follow up questions. The key is to deftly but seriously challenge their reason(s), and compel the client make the case for moving forward.

Another effective approach is to state that "We're at a point where we need to evaluate and confirm the process so far," followed by some specific probing questions. Maybe you bring your sales manager along as the bad cop to "evaluate your sales skills and grasp of the client requirements."

Or bring a senior executive to help, previously coached on the sales objective and armed with specific questions about where things stand from proposal, contracting or timing perspectives. In this scenario, I might let the client in on my executive's style beforehand and mention that the questions could be direct and even confrontational. In this way, the client is prepared for the worst (which never materializes) and can accurately represent where the deal stands.

If, during the prep call with the client, it becomes clear that the deal isn't where it should be, there is no longer reason to get my executive involved, and a potential career-limiting disaster has been avoided.

In any case, your approach need not be negative nor condescending. Rather, simply show a genuine curiosity about understanding the problem. Make the statement or ask the question. Then sit back and wait. Don't sell. And don't flinch.

Yes, actively trying to kill your deal is a little like jumping out of an airplane. Terrifying. But if the plane is on fire and plummeting downwards, you'll need to jump eventually. Freeing yourself from a plummeting deal is equally lifesaving.

Get ready to jump.

Paint the Picture

Assumptions can be a dangerous thing.

I recently had a follow up sales call with marketing people at one of the premier health systems in the country. Both individuals were super sharp, knew their stuff and were particularly innovative. I knew this having attended their respective presentations at a conference just a month prior to our web call. In advance of the call, I'd sent along some background material on my company and a couple emails meant to keep us top of mind and reinforce some key points.

Given this particular audience, my strategy was to quickly review the materials previously sent and explain what it was that my company did. Once the stage was set, my thinking was that the conversation would then flow and these two marketing geniuses would ask their probing questions, make some suggestions, and then ultimately land on a potential pilot or experiment of their own clever design.

My assumption was that this particular audience, given their company's market size and reputation, wouldn't respond well to being told that they should just sign up for 'the standard package.' Instead, I thought it best to keep things conceptual and without specific boundaries for what a relationship might be, given that my company is a tiny start-up and any relationship with these guys would be worth pursuing.

I was wrong.

While the call wasn't a complete disaster (as I write this, we're still in active sales mode with them), the conversation floundered. I got meandering questions about our web traffic. They wondered how we engage consumers. I found myself forced to explain esoteric, trivial details about our platform far afield from where I thought any meaningful collaboration might have been headed. Basically, I'd squandered the opportunity. And I'd wasted their time.

The lesson that I had to relearn here was that my assumption was woefully naïve. I'd expected a lively, productive brainstorming session, but what this prospective customer needed were boundaries. And they always do. Customers need a frame of reference. Rather than being constrictive, having one or more defined choices gives the customer a baseline or foundation within which to work.

You need to paint the picture. Provide the vision and show them the way. Maybe your customer will say no, or deviate from the path you're suggesting, but you're giving them parameters. Maybe they get creative and want to color outside the lines, but they can only do that if you first give them the lines. Be consultative, of course, but give them choices. Not 'the sky's the limit.'

Because, as I just painfully relearned, "We're proposing that you start with…" is invariably a better sales strategy than "We're leaving this entirely up to you."

Five Great Books on Sales (That Aren't Sales Books)

1. *The Innovators Dilemma* by Clay Christiansen – Because the only constant is change.

2. *Crossing the Chasm* by Geoffrey Moore – You need to know who you should be selling to.

3. *The Next Economy* by Paul Hawken – Why this book isn't more highly regarded is a mystery.

4. *The War of Art* by Steven Pressfield – We're all artists, and the real enemy is within.

5. *Man's Search for Meaning* by Viktor Frankl – Because every now and again, it helps to have perspective.

Selling... or Buying?

Here's something to think about. In one of Seth Godin's many brilliant blog posts* he talks about how things are either bought or sold. As a business person, it's important to understand the difference because there's more to it than marketing and awareness. Being adept at understanding the specific drivers behind buying and selling will considerably enhance the direction and shape of your career, your brand and your expertise.

Notably important to those of us carrying a bag, the compensation is typically different when people are buying from when you're selling. Things that need to be sold lead to greater compensation than things that get bought. Obviously. If you're just taking orders or standing behind the register, there may be plenty of marketing at work but probably very little real selling required.

In the opposite extreme, when the item is expensive, complicated, rare or optional, the rewards for getting the sale usually are commensurate with the greater sales effort required.

Why does this matter? For a professional salesperson, the ideal job is at a company where 'things are bought,' but the structure, staff and compensation are built with a 'things are sold' mindset. In this latter instance, there exists some brief but wonderous window of time when the company and its product have taken off but the compensation plan hasn't yet had time to catch up. Think relational databases in the 1980's, SAP and PeopleSoft in the 1990's and maybe Salesforce in the early 2000's. It's great while it lasts but, sadly, it seldom lasts long enough.

Alas, in this hyper-competitive world, those wild but lucrative rides are harder to find, and they run their course more quickly and unpredictably. (In lieu of this, there is the possibility of pre-IPO stock, but divining the potential value and likelihood of a meaningful liquidity event is crystal ball territory.)

A more reliable career strategy is to find yourself wherever you are and then invest in your development, your skills and your reputation. Because while they say it's better to be lucky than good, being good is the one thing you can control.

* http://sethgodin.typepad.com/seths_blog/2012/01/sold-or-bought.html

When Winning Isn't

There are deals you shouldn't win.

Just as there are bad movies, bad restaurants and bad spouses, there are bad customers. Impossible to work with, slow to pay, constantly reorganizing, certain to oversee a failed implementation, untrustworthy, etc., etc. As difficult as it may be to walk away from any sales opportunity, there are definitely situations where you're better off losing. Or not even competing.

Back when I was selling on Wall Street, I was in the hunt for a big project for a large financial services company. Under normal circumstances, we had a legitimate shot. But the RFP was miserably long and onerous, the customer was belligerent and caustic (even by Wall Street standards), and they had a longstanding reputation for being notoriously slow to pay.

As the customer's selection process dragged along, we did our own internal evaluation. Did it make sense to jump through the various hoops that the prospects set for us? Not really. Did we see significant additional business coming out of this relationship? Again, not likely, as the company was highly siloed and cross-selling into other divisions would take more of the same tedious effort. Did we enjoy working with their team? And did we trust them? Again, no and no. These answers prompted some serious soul-searching.

Ultimately, we 'lost' the deal. At a certain point in their evaluation process, we simply realized that it wasn't worth the aggravation. We politely withdrew and wished them success. (Wall Street, like most verticals, is surprisingly small and tight-knit. Those on the selection team would inevitably turn up at other firms and be making other purchasing decisions. We calculated that making a deft and graceful exit would be the best potential outcome.)

From both the company's perspective and my own, it was a tough decision. It's hard to turn away from potential revenue and the corresponding commission payouts. And we thought that adding a big brand name to our client list would have been a coup. (In retrospect, not so much, as one of their contract restrictions prohibited us from mentioning them in marketing materials or using them as a reference.)

But the benefits from taking ourselves out of the race weren't insignificant, either. Imagine the wasted time chasing down accounts receivables or dealing with poor references, or the suffering that comes with adversarial contract disputes over tedious tasks you would gladly perform as part of normal customer service.

The vendor evaluation experience is a reliable indicator of the future relationship. Who wants years of that kind of misery? Instead, that time and energy would now be available to invest in better, more valuable relationships and projects. Or playing golf. Plus, in doing so we were able to burden a competitor with a miserable, resource-sucking, perpetually dissatisfied customer.

It's never easy to say "no." Walking away from a deal flies in the face of what the entire sales mentality is supposedly about. But it pays to recognize bad deals and bad customers when you see them. It may not feel like winning at the time, but sometimes the best battle is the one you avoid, and the chance to fight another day.

Top Five Tips for Customer Golf

1. Carry cash – For tips, bets, snack cart.

2. Bet at your peril (and if you must, keep the wagers small.)

3. Just because the customer trash talks doesn't mean you can.

4. Wear sunscreen.

5. You can be a huge sales success without ever playing customer golf.

It's About Triangulation

As any given sales opportunity gets bigger, more strategic or expands across multiple divisions, it inevitably becomes more complicated to manage and more difficult to close. Every new variable brings with it the possibility of more potential, but also greater risk of loss or delay.

Among the potential headaches you should anticipate include:

- New players and organizations that come into the picture.
- Different budgets and purchasing rules that come into effect.
- New legal and contracting constraints that need to be addressed and mitigated.

These added factors make navigating to a successful outcome more difficult. (They also make things more interesting, but that's a topic for another day.) Fundamental to reaching that successful outcome is an ability to anticipate, respond and guide the sale based on all these new and competing perspectives.

Your ability to step back and think about the deal from the perspective of the various decisionmakers and influencers, one at a time, is a skill worth developing. Because the particular motivation for one constituent in the deal is often inconsistent with another, even if they're in the same division or department, you need to weigh and address these different perspectives. To accurately understand and appreciate each person's purchasing motivations, you need to be able to *triangulate*.

Triangulation, from a sales standpoint, is the concept of engaging with a broad, informed and influential group of contacts within a given account and then validating amongst them in order to determine the organizational (sales) reality.

The key assumption is that you've identified all of the decisionmakers and influencers in the deal. You also must be actively engaged with them individually and with adequate frequency. *Individually* because you want direct, candid and critical feedback. *Adequate frequency* because the sales situation is likely to be even more fluid, biased and fraught with political undercurrents than your run-of-the-mill sale. (Most big, expensive and strategic decisions are. Turf is being challenged, departments are being rewarded or punished, and organization/power structures can pivot significantly on the outcome of these deals.)

When selling to a large bank, I had a respectable license contract set to close during our third quarter. But in the process of doing my usual 'selling by wandering around,' a discussion with another division manager found them eager to jump onto the deal. As such software sales go, adding this this new group to the previous deal would decrease the per license price as the total contract value increased. In theory, everyone comes out ahead. So far, so good.

But the larger deal, now involving two different divisions, became a more complicated one for various reasons. Some of the software would be deployed in their foreign branches, which required a new contract review and a rash of edits and more legal work. The product mix wasn't completely consistent between the two divisions, causing changes to the price schedule. Finally, new approval processes were required that added to the delay, jeopardizing what had now become a December 31 signature under the best of circumstances. (The contract actually became even messier because my company's various international sales teams learned where many of these licenses were to be deployed and started angling for commission credit.)

To orchestrate all these moving parts required staying in ongoing conversation with the various technical, management and trading groups involved in each of the divisions. One of the takeaways was that it was easier and more insightful to have a quick series of individual conversations than try to coordinate group status calls. More importantly, these one-on-one updates positioned me as a reliable communication channel between these quasi-competitive divisions.

This process enabled me to monitor the pulse of the sale as it dragged its way slowly into December. Despite these complexities, the delay remained manageable and all the deal terms were settled and executive approvals completed with a small cushion to spare. After a complex and protracted sales journey, I was assured that a purchase order for the entire contract could be expected any day.

But the fax machine sat idle and the purchase order didn't materialize. Instead, I was told there would be a meeting with the vice president of purchasing scheduled for the last week of December. It was a formality, I'd been reassured. This purchasing executive made it a point of meeting the vendors whenever a contract exceeded a certain dollar threshold. I briefed my sales manager and we headed downtown to say hello and wish the VP a happy holiday.

But this VP had other ideas. After brief pleasantries, he explained that the purchase wasn't approved and wouldn't be unless we dropped the price by another ten percent. The specific threat was that this deal wasn't going to happen if we didn't comply *and* that they'd go with our direct competitor instead.

So here we are. It's the last week of the fiscal year with an enormous contract hanging in the balance. I'm stuck in the impressive corner office of some executive issuing a plausible threat, pondering whether to acquiesce to the demand for an additional price cut. (A curious thing about software sales is that every extra dollar is essentially pure profit, so that the whole dynamic of discounting has a weird, theoretical feel to it. Thus, giving in on price isn't the same when there's no direct 'raw material cost of sale.' Or at least that's how software salespeople often see the problem.)

Except that we didn't acquiesce.

Because we knew we didn't have to. We knew that their engineering teams had already started developing, that the trading desks liked the functionality and that management had already bought off on the proposal.

Most importantly, we knew that they had serious production deadlines that would be jeopardized by a change in software. We even knew that the ten percent shake-down this VP was attempting was trivial compared the cost of any delay. (You can't fault the guy for trying, though. As is often the case, he was measured and bonused based on how much savings he could squeeze out of vendors like us.)

Instead, I explained that we already negotiated the deal, had assurances from the business heads that the proposal was acceptable and that they were ready to move forward. "We're sorry, but we can't help you out here." What followed was a tense back-and-forth conversation about pricing, other vendors, and rebidding the project. Finally, he wrapped up our meeting with a blunt statement that he wouldn't be able to approve the deal. That it was effectively dead.

With the full backing of my boss, I chose to hang tough through the negotiation for two reasons: principle and money. Principle because we'd already negotiated in good faith with the senior executives that had the approval authority. I wanted to avoid undermining their reputations if some purchasing functionary bullied us into a different arrangement. And money because that ten percent loss in revenue was all commission overrides. Let's just say it was significant.

A cloud hung over the rest of the holiday season as I'd effectively traded a deal that would have assured me hitting my quota for one that, theoretically, would have put me into some very attractive accelerators and propelled me into the annual sales club. Now I was looking at neither.

For the waning few days of the quarter I kept in touch with clients while wrapping up the typical year-end purchase orders. I also had now begrudgingly resigned myself to the realization that that my huge strategic win had flatlined.

And it was verifiably dead, until the morning of December 31st, when the fax machine kicked on and that glorious purchase order came through. For the full contract value.

While I'd like to say I knew all along that our take-it-or-leave-it strategy was a winner, mostly I felt like I'd dodged a bullet.

Still, it also felt good to be right. But being right wouldn't have been possible if I hadn't been triangulating among everyone involved and knew the situation from every important perspective. And the only way to do that is through lots of conversations with lots of different people and asking lots of different questions. Questions like:

- What happens if this deal goes through? And if it doesn't?

- How is the proposal being received?

- Where is the funding coming from? Is it one source or many?

- Who stands to gain (or lose) from this new initiative?

- What effect is there on staff, territory, status?

- Does anyone benefit/suffer from this decision (versus a different one, for example)?

Again, every deal is won in the day-to-day execution. It's in these individual conversations where the selling really takes place, and it's where your sale will either flourish or die. Skip these conversations and avoid thinking about how everything triangulates among those that have a stake in the outcome at your peril. Break it all down and that's what makes the whole thing challenging, interesting and rewarding.

And fun.

Five Memorable (and Printable) Sales Management Quotes *

1. "People will write things in an email that they'd never have the stones to say to your face."

2. "That deal was so bad, he should have played golf that day instead."

3. "You know, saying 'Performance up to 80% faster also includes *slower*.'"

4. "If you already knew you were going with our competition, why are we even here?!"

5. "I've been doing this since they were making 'em outta wood."

* What are yours? Please send them to brendan@brendanmcadams.com

It Should be Fun

Work should be fun. (Say it out loud, like a mantra, to yourself, over and over.) Sales should be satisfying, rewarding and even fun. You should enjoy what you're doing. You should find satisfaction and challenge in the discipline of sales, in the process, and in working with customers.

Certainly, there are pressures and stress. There are unpleasant clients and moments of frustration. There are failures and setbacks, too. Of course, every job or endeavor carries this risk. But if you're not enjoying yourself most of the time, you're probably not doing it right.

To do it right, you need to make the job your own. The job has to be complementary to you and your identity. You need it to fit.

This is both easier and more difficult than it seems. It's easy in the sense that you simply make the job and how you execute it consistent with who you are.

It's more difficult because you're up against the well-established pressure to conform to the culture of whatever your peers, company, management and industry dictate. After all, you can't be a wild and crazy sales machine in the staid, buttoned-down world of surgical implants or amongst the green eye-shade types in financial services.

Or maybe you can. That's up to you to figure out. It's surprising how many wacky, creative, undefinable (and successful) salespeople are able to thrive on their own terms in industries as boring and hidebound as defense contracting or manufacturing.

My corporate sales experience started in telecommunications and financial services before ending up in healthcare, the latter being an industry that might have a near-monopoly on the dry, detailed and mundane. (Spend some time understanding revenue cycle management, patient billing, or clinical trials and you'll know what I'm talking about.) And yet there are plenty of successful sales professionals who walk (dance, skip, strut?) to the beat of their own unconventional drum.

Admittedly, this takes a measure of courage and self-confidence to pull off. You're battling conformity and the status quo, so expect resistance. But the rewards, both psychic and financial, are worth the initial discomfort, most of which is imaginary.

And let's be practical. If this is something you're going to dedicate yourself to, you might as well make it fun.

Here's the fascinating part: Your customers want to enjoy their time with you. Most people want to work with interesting people. It's fun for them. Few things enliven and improve the numbing tedium of the average customer's day like a refreshing blast of authentic, creative enthusiasm from someone genuinely dedicated to their personal and business success. So be on the lookout for fun.

I've been to baseball games and car races with clients, events that are squarely in my wheelhouse. (Maybe my favorite baseball experience was seeing the Durham Bulls play just after the movie came out, and that's true even having been to the World Series.) But I've also been to rodeos and local museums and high school football games with customers, all of which have been great adventures.

During the tail end of one particular sales call in Florida, my customer explained that the space shuttle was launching that afternoon. I responded like a nerdy 5th grader…"Really? That would be cool to see!" To which he said, "Well, let's go then." And we did. He even packed sandwiches and beer.

Hit the top restaurants when you travel, or the ones Guy Fiery discovers. When in Baltimore make your customer go duckpin bowling, check out the airplane 'boneyard' in Tucson, and visit the Eisenhower Presidential Museum if you find yourself in Kansas City.

You don't need to show up at the client's office in a clown suit or sing your voicemail messages, but this job should be fun. Again, if it's not, you're not doing it right.

Ease into it. Begin simply. Give thought to who you are, what you stand for (or can stand) and what might be different or out of the ordinary. What would your job look like if it were more like you thought it should be? Armed with that awareness, add whatever ingredients to your selling style that will make it more satisfying, more real and more authentically you.

Trust me. It'll be fun.

Practice Effortlessness

Just because selling is hard doesn't mean you have to make it look that way.

Yes, there is a chance that you'll elicit customer sympathy by being rushed, disorganized and overwhelmed. That's the world we live in. But it's just as likely that you'll be regarded as underpowered, unreliable, unprepared, or otherwise not up to the task. Just because the customer is flustered, behind schedule, dysfunctional, or otherwise in a state of never-ending chaos doesn't mean they want their vendor partner to be that way.

What your client needs is partners to surround themselves with and align with that make things easier, more enjoyable and more profitable. And that lessen the risk in the bargain.

Part of being one of those select few is to look like you know what you're doing. And getting your client to see you as capable and professional requires you to make everything look easy.

The first step to be aware. The simple act of examining how you're going about what you're doing is the place to start. Notice your pace, your tone of voice, how you carry yourself. Take a breath. Relax. Remember that this job should be fun, or at least satisfying.

Next, make things easy on yourself. That means having tools, resources, people, dates and times, etc. ready when you need them. Plans and strategy can change in the heat of the battle, but having the right tools at your immediate disposal are both confidence-building and enabling. (See page 49.)

If you can draw quickly from an already stocked warehouse of tools, effortlessness takes less effort. If you've got a guy back at HQ that can fix a support issue with one phone call, your burden just got lighter. Similarly, knowing someone that's a wizard with PowerPoint is like gold. Developing that team of people and assemblage of resources takes time. But the payoff is huge for both you and your customers.

Once that's in place, then you just have to figure out how to make it look like it's second nature. Image is everything, or at least it counts for a lot. Visualize success. Imagine yourself being smooth and patient. This might seem basic and obvious, or even unnecessary, but it bears consideration. Great athletes play the big game out over and over in their heads before they ever step onto the playing field. In exactly the same way, professional salespeople know how to project themselves as calm, composed and professional.

For the record, effortlessness didn't come easily for me. I'm something of a 'scrambler,' and capable of waiting until the last minute to get things done. To combat that tendency and make things easier on myself, I try to follow up quickly. I aim for more, shorter meetings. And I'm constantly trying squeeze time out of the sales cycle. These practices help take the pressure off and makes it easier for me to *seem* like I have it all under control.

Because customers expect it. They do not want to engage with someone stiff and robotic, or someone stressed out and disorganized. They expect the person that is you, but an effortless version of you.

Before your sales call, spend a few minutes in mental rehearsal. Walk through how you want the meeting to go. What's the ideal outcome? What needs to happen to achieve that outcome? How does it feel? Conduct your mental pre-game ritual and see the outcome in your mind before it happens.

Finally, manage your commitments. Be scrupulous when customers ask for things that require tremendous effort. That's not to say that you shouldn't volunteer. But be selective and discerning.

Don't make the mistake of committing to a request for something you shouldn't commit to. It's easy to do but worth applying the discipline to seriously evaluate the ask. (See page 123.) I've seen countless salespeople (including me, more times than I care to count) promise to follow up on some pointless task brought up by a prospect, usually not even remotely critical to the deal.

Ultimately, it's all part of the performance. As hard as the job may be at times, don't make it look that way.

Make it look easy.

About Marketing

Most companies' marketing departments (with the help of data, AI, and a broad sweep of software and tools) have made great strides at customizing and tailoring the marketing message to better meet the specific interests of each prospective consumer. That trend will no doubt continue, bringing with it a genuine reckoning for many sales professionals as the move towards more self-service further reduces the scope of direct sales. (But that's a topic for another day, and a different book.)

That said, the effective salesperson will continue to have value so long as marketing efforts can't fully personalize and inform the buying experience and process as much as prospective customers will demand. (This is another argument to support the old saw that that the weaker your marketing, the stronger your sales effort and/or product need to be.) Which is to say that good sale people aren't obsolete. Yet.

As important as market awareness and regular prospect contact is, it is unlikely that a new deal will appear in the pipeline thanks to any blog post or 'blast' email campaign. An eight-page white paper won't help a prospective client recognize their need for your solution if they don't read it. Nor will a generic video with animated stock figures and thought bubbles that rattle off a feature list but gloss over the implementation process required.

A good marketing team will work hand-in-glove with sales to make sure that strategy and tactics are well defined and appropriate for the target audience, providing the air cover to effectively support your sales efforts on the ground. But lately, the collective marketing mindset seems to have morphed to accept the notion that marketing is now ~90% of the sales cycle, with the actual sales team needed only the to wrap up the nasty loose ends. With that perspective, certain problems arise:

- You reduce direct client input, replaced by feedback collected by marketing efforts.
- The mentality of 'more is better,' and with that a greater pace and volume of messaging and content.
- The dominance of Google and Facebook, and the insatiable demand for fresh content, drive the priorities. Marketing goals are more focused on engagement and SEO and less aligned with sales goals.

So, what can you do about this?

Mostly, it's doing what you're already doing. Ask questions, understand the client's business, their competitors, and the issues driving their decision process. Then be proactive and generous with what you learn, sharing it marketing team early and often. Basically, you're helping marketing when you:

- **Collect real-world client case studies** – Get clients to explain how they use your product. Good data points include things like implementation time/effort required, ROI/break-even, reduction in turn-around time, increased market share/sales, etc. These can turn into full-blown campaigns, but at a minimum the folks back in HQ are getting real-world insight.

- **Solicit customer feedback** – How are clients and prospects hearing about your company or product? What do they think? Did they read the last white paper? What did they think of the last webinar? What would they like to see? What are other vendors doing? The insights you gain can help your marketing counterparts craft better tools and events.

  As one example, a recent consulting engagement had me working with orthopedic surgeons. The feedback I gathered was that doctors couldn't dedicate the time to watch a 45 minute video. In response, marketing pivoted by creating short bulleted emails, lightly formatted and incorporating supporting data.

- **Solicit references** – Recruit your happy clients to volunteer to talk to the press, and then loop in your marketing team. These are big wins for your marketing brethren, and as the sales pro you're better positioned to make it happen.

- **Volunteer** – Offer to review draft marketing material and content and provide quick feedback. Shag down a client quote. Act as guinea pig for their next campaign. Being active in the process may add to your workload, but it's the best way to get the marketing support you need when you need it.

You're ultimately tasked with establishing and nurturing the client relationship, so be aware of what the marketing team is sending out, understand the material and, most importantly, do what you can to make it worthwhile. An unspoken part of the job is to protect the client. After all, they're your customer. And you're their advocate, and that responsibility starts before you even meet or speak with them.

Despite focus groups and opt-ins, click-throughs and web surveys, the customer-sales relationship remains the best, richest and most consistent channel to understand the customer and address their needs.

That's your channel. Don't neglect it.

Telling Stories

The Apollo space program is universally regarded as one of man's great achievements, and simultaneously a marvel of complexity. And yet, those involved with the program at the onset basically simplified the entire endeavor into three key goals:

1. Send a man to the moon;

2. Get him back safely to Earth; and

3. Do it by the end of 1969.

A huge, unimaginably difficult task distilled down to three simple, digestible objectives. Of course, any big, worthwhile endeavor benefits from a simple, well-defined set of objectives. Such a vision works to keep the focus and motivation on the tasks at hand, whether it be beating the Russians to the moon or exceeding your annual sales quota.

That's a story. It's a true story, and summarized to the bone, but it makes a point. Stories sell. They draw you, engage you, and paint a picture. And ideally, the pictures you paint help your clients see a brighter, more successful future as a result of selecting your solution.

I actually sat in on a longer version of that story, told by a director at Bell Labs, who used the Apollo program as a roadmap for the important project they had facing them. The details of that meeting remain vivid almost thirty years later, which had to do with the rate of innovation and the impact it had on NASA's launch strategy. It worked to make their project objective concrete and understandable – and inspiring by virtue of being wrapped up in the mythology of the space program.

Stories sell. Anthropologists and psychologists will tell you that this is because we're a tribal species accustomed to learning around the campfire or the kitchen table from family, friends or tribal elders. It's in our culture and our community. Physicians and neuroscientists can more specifically explain that the brain has evolved to encourage and support certain synaptic relationships, that stories and storytelling are hard-coded right into our DNA.

Ultimately, stories sell because they deliver information to us in a format we're comfortable with and easy to process. They capture our interest because we don't know where we're being taken or how things will end. There's an element of expectation that a good story creates, whether it's the possibility of learning something new or just seeing that same thing from a fresh angle. (For example, I hadn't previously appreciated that you could simplify the Apollo space program down to three simple objectives.)

How can you weave stories into your sales repertoire? Consider your style and delivery. What can work authentically for you, and what wouldn't? Collect examples from other industries and draw parallels. Read about things outside your industry. You can easily draw from history, and technology folks love a good science reference.

The dogged determination of the intrepid inventor making the earth-shattering discovery after innumerable setbacks is a winner in almost any crowd. But remember to keep it fresh, and ideally even surprising. How Thomas Edison invented the light bulb is now tired ground. (Besides, the guy was an SOB and is more revered than he deserves.) Instead, a story that weaves in Lewis Howard Lattimer, a black inventor who developed the carbon filaments that made the light bulb possible, would be unexpected and thus interesting.

Sports anecdotes are reliable territory, of course, but they quickly become cliché and aren't meaningful to every audience. But an exception might include a little-known anecdote about the trials and ultimate victory of a local sports team that demonstrates your interest and investment in the client's community.

A good story shouldn't feel like a sales pitch. It comes at you obliquely and gracefully. Ideally, it doesn't have anything directly to do with what you're selling. And if it's about you, it pays to be humble and self-deprecating.

A good story should also adhere to a few other guidelines. It shouldn't preach or lecture, and it should probably steer clear of subjects fraught with dodgy subject matter: sex, drugs, current politics. (You know...all the fun topics.) Clearly, you need to know your audience.

Most importantly, it shouldn't drag on. To resonate, it needs to keep your audience engaged, so move them efficiently to the big finish.

And a big finish is critical. Your story should have meaning, and should connect them in some way to the shared objectives that you will achieve together.

Finally, telling a good story takes practice, and even a little courage to pull off. Like any skill, being able to tell a compelling, engaging stem-winder that has people waiting eagerly for its ending takes practice. Test it out. Conduct a few auditions. Perhaps practice on your friends or family or at a dinner party before you inflict it on a prospect.

That said, your stories can be about anything. They can be about you, or your dog, or a friend's bad summer job. They don't even have to be true.

They just need to be true enough.

The Big Night

One of the more underrated and underused perks that come with a big win is the celebratory dinner. To get to this point, there have been weeks or months of work and tension and probably some confrontation, with lots of players involved and lots of expectations set. After the relief (or resignation) that comes with a signed agreement, you need to change the collective mood. It's time for a reset.

I propose 'The Big Night.' Best executed shortly after the deal is signed, it's a chance to get the respective customer and vendor teams together for an official congratulations, thank you, and 'we can't wait to get started' dinner.

Oddly, this is a rare event. Customers don't get to experience an official kick-off or thank you dinner often enough, and this is especially true for the folks in the trenches. A relaxing, celebratory event creates a great initial bond between the organizations that can help keep things on track through any tense and sticky post-signature rocky spot before real progress is visible and momentum is established.

I've done a bunch of these and they've always been huge fun. One particularly memorable celebratory bash involved a stressful sprint from Boston to New York City to be there. It should have been an easy flight with time to spare, but unpredictable East Coast weather had me switch to Amtrak and a soggy slog through Greenwich Village to make it in time. (Try to hail a cab in a New York City downpour.)

I finally arrived drenched and forty-five minutes late. Fortunately, the evening festivities were just picking up speed. A boisterous and animated evening played out for the next several hours, with too many wine bottles to count, behind-the-scenes stories about the sales process, and photos taken of the ridiculous bill. That dinner would come up in conversations years later with intense fondness. More importantly, it bonded the two groups together and kept the project on track when obstacles inevitably arose.

We're not talking about pizza in the conference room, but it doesn't need to be flamboyant. It does need to be meaningful and special. The Big Night should include as many of the right players from both the customer and the vendor side of the initiative as practical. Ideally, you want people from all levels of both companies. And it shouldn't be about work.

Pick a venue that provides a distraction, but nothing too rustic or you risk losing senior executives. (Orchestrating a chance to have the troops mingle with their senior management is something that scores huge points). A restaurant is probably the best and easiest. Ideally, get a private dining room. Consider group chemistry. If it helps to include a couple extra fun people from either side to make the whole event more engaging, do it.

Plan to say a few words. Do it early, before too much celebrating occurs. You will want to say "Thank you" for being selected, of course, but use the time to recognize individual contributions and effort on both sides.

Stress the team's excitement at the promise of a successful project and a long and happy relationship. Give your client executive the opportunity to speak, with advanced warning. Then encourage people to meet and mingle and congratulate themselves for a job well done. At that point, step back and let the evening play out. Because you've done your part.

Five Things Customers Never Say

1. "I wish there were more slides."

2. "We have an unlimited budget."

3. "I've got all day."

4. "No…Really…You go ahead."

5. "We're not looking at anybody else."

Thank You

Thank you for reading this book.

Feels good to hear it, doesn't it? Who doesn't enjoy the chance to be recognized for their contribution? And while it's obvious, I feel compelled to reinforce this most basic social lubricant.

Say "thank you."

Say it early and often. Make it second nature and genuine. Thank administrative assistants for scheduling appointments, tracking down projectors, getting you a conference room and whatever else it is that they do to make your job easier. Thank your product manager for shifting her staff meeting to be available for that key demonstration. Thank the unappreciated person managing the front desk for, well, whatever.

A simple card with two sentences is all it takes. (See page 61.) Or a Starbucks $5 gift card. (I try to keep a bunch of them in my bag for these opportunities. But cash works, too.) For the unappreciated hotel staffer that gets you the clutch dinner reservation, or the administrative assistant that perfectly handles all the 'big meeting' logistics, or for the guy in marketing put the beautiful finishing touches on a key proposal. Say "Thank you."

It's common courtesy, of course. But it's also smart. Nobody gets thanked often enough.

Nobody.

Loose Ends

Loose Ends

Closing remarks, resources and thank you's.
Lots of thank you's.

Final Thoughts

Writing a book is hard.

Or at least it was for me. It requires tremendous effort, and despite the effort can feel like you aren't getting closer to the finish. It's a slog. Even when it's finished, sent off to the printing shop to be solidified in black and white, the work still isn't over. Because now you need to let people know. You need to get out there, talk it up, promote and evangelize.

Plus, there's the self-doubt that inevitably seeps in at the most inopportune moments. Writing a book means you're spending a lot of time alone, thinking and typing, which gives your psyche plenty of opportunity to wonder what it is you think you're doing, question why it matters, and point out where the flaws are. And there are lots of flaws...

Which is to say, writing a book is just like life. And like sales. Ultimately, you need to love the grind, the process, and the little details. Because the secret to writing a book, to being good at sales, and the secret to life is pretty much the same.

You need to keep at it.

For as long as I can remember, my father has had certain pithy observations that would get repeated at the most appropriate (or inappropriate) moment. One of which is particularly applicable in almost every situation. "Don't let the bastards get you down."

Which is perhaps the most useful and indisputable advice among these pages. Just keep at it. Practice. Learn. Try out new ideas. And get incrementally better.

Most important, disregard the bastards.

Next Steps

Thank you for reading! I hope you're able to find some useful ideas to try out and enhance your sales skillset. And if you can, please add a short review on Amazon and let me know what you thought.

Also, visit www.brendanmcadams.com to get access to the forms and materials mentioned.

Finally, send along an email if you have questions, want to discuss sales philosophies, or disagree with me(?!) My email is brendan@brendanmcadams.com and please connect with me on LinkedIn.

Sales Craft

Acknowledgments

If there's any value to be found within these pages, it's due to the wisdom, guidance, observation and patience shown to me by so many. (The blame for everything else should be directed entirely at me.)

Of course, I need to thank many customers from over the years from whom I've learned so much about sales, business and relationships. Thanks in particular to Tom Dwyer, Curt Wilber, Tom Pellegrino, Rick Lee, Joe Hollander, Len Camarda, Steve Cohan, John Ginelli, Rick Shinto, Zinnia Santiago, Dr. Mike Siegel, Dave Terry, Tony Cheng, Tony Schueth, Brad Kogan, Jim Eppel, Bill Fandrich, Hsin Kan, Brett Coleman, Barb Derian, Dr. Amy Ladd, Michiko Tanabe, David Perry, Dr. Kam Kalantar, Dr. Alpesh Amin, George Wenning, Kim LaPietra, Dr. Robert Weinreb, Prof. Marco Ferrari, Bob

Allen, and Dr. Jeffrey Kang.

And I've benefited from the guidance and company of many really fine executives, sales managers and fellow salespeople over the course of my career. Thanks to: Jim Fleming, Larry Arata, Tim Milovich, Bob Aloisio, Ron Alvarez, Jeff Verney, Nancy Ham, Tim Tolan, Mike Long, Terry Yanni, Philip Lay, Bob Farley, Jim LoPresti, Gary Stuart, Ed Graham, Ken Lowe, Bill Appelgate, Phil White, Philippe Kahn, Karen Thompson, Scott Miller, Tony DeCicco, Rick Altinger, Mike Taber, and Ben Gardner.

I've wanted to write a book for as long as I can remember, but it was Tim Tolan that got this started and pushed me along. His encouragement and advice have been invaluable over the years.

This book wouldn't have happened without the reliable and steadfast encouragement from John Marron, Joe Valenti, and Adam Budish. Each of them suffered through my excuses and explanations, provided inexhaustible optimism and thoughtful feedback, and nudged me gently but insistently forward.

Bob Graham has been invaluable as editor, advisor, critic and coach. Our regular 'coffee and consultation' sessions made this book infinitely better, and I'm already looking forward to the next project.

My good friend and Expertscape co-founder, Dr. John Sotos, has been an indefatigable source of creativity, enthusiasm and rationality. Our lengthy conversations have informed much of this book.

Of course, I'm especially grateful to my parents. I've been gifted with love, support, encouragement and an environment rich with opportunity and freedom. I've been spoiled rotten in all the best possible ways.

Finally, I want to thank Lorri White, the love of my life and center of my universe. She has endured it all and has kept me on a sure and steady course throughout. We made it!

Thank you, everyone.

Sales Craft

About the Author

Brendan McAdams is a sales and marketing professional focused on B2B clients in healthcare. He is the cofounder of Expertscape.com, the premiere system for identifying and objectively ranking medical expertise by specific topic, condition or diagnosis. He also operates a consulting practice that helps healthcare technology companies market and sell to risk-bearing entities. (e.g. health insurance companies, health systems and large physician groups.)

And when he's not working with health care clients, you can probably find him in his shop making chips and sawdust.

www.brendanmcadams.com

Sales Craft

Made in the USA
Middletown, DE
26 September 2019